Phillis Wheatley and the Romantics

Phillis Wheatley and the Romantics

John C. Shields

The University of Tennessee Press • Knoxville

Copyright © 2010 by The University of Tennessee Press / Knoxville.
All Rights Reserved. Manufactured in the United States of America.
First Edition.

The paper in this book meets the requirements of American National Standards Institute / National Information Standards Organization specification Z39.48-1992 (Permanence of Paper). It contains 30 percent post-consumer waste and is certified by the Forest Stewardship Council.

Library of Congress Cataloging-in-Publication Data

Shields, John C., 1944–
Phillis Wheatley and the Romantics / John C. Shields. — 1st ed.
    p. cm.
Includes bibliographical references and index.
ISBN-13: 978-1-57233-705-3 (alk. paper)
ISBN-10: 1-57233-705-2 (alk. paper)
1. Wheatley, Phillis, 1753–1784—Criticism and interpretation.
2. Wheatley, Phillis, 1753–1784—Influence.
3. American literature—African American authors—History and criticism.
4. Romanticism.
I. Title.

PS866.W5Z696 2010
811'.1—dc22   2009039644

For their constant belief in me, this book is dedicated to
Russell Rutter
and
Alvin C. Bowman

Contents

Preface	ix
Acknowledgments	xi
Chapter 1. Before Wheatley: The Imagination from Plato to Bruno	1
Chapter 2. Before Wheatley: The Imagination from Bruno to William Billings	19
Chapter 3. Wheatley's "Long Poem" and Subsequent Considerations	45
Chapter 4. After Wheatley: In England, France, and Germany, Excluding Kant	65
Chapter 5. Kant and Wheatley	85
Chapter 6. Wheatley and Coleridge	97
Concluding Remarks: Is Wheatley the Progenetrix of Romanticism?	115
Postscript: What Remains to Be Done	121
Chronology	123
Works Cited and Consulted	125
Index	135

Preface

This monograph extends the argument of *Phillis Wheatley's Poetics of Liberation: Backgrounds and Contexts,* which holds that Wheatley is a largely misunderstood yet brilliant author. The objective of this and the earlier text is to ascertain the value of Wheatley's works, along with their multi-layered meanings. Surprisingly, a productive and provocative result of acknowledging the value of Wheatley's texts leads us to learn that, at least during the later years of the eighteenth and the early years of the nineteenth centuries, her poems prove to have been more appealing to many intellectuals in Great Britain and the Continent than they were to Early Americans.

In short, *Phillis Wheatley and the Romantics* traces a heretofore unrecognized impact that certain of Wheatley's texts, particularly her "Long Poem," consisting of "On Recollection," "Thoughts on the Works of Providence," and "On Imagination," exercised in the shaping of what we have come to call the several romanticisms. While not all authors named herein (e.g. Kant, Blumenbach, Imlay, and Clarkson) were romantics, certainly Wordsworth, Coleridge, DeQuincey, and Keats fall into this category. Never at any time do I presume in this tract to define romanticism. What I have attempted to demonstrate is how remarkably certain of Wheatley's poems participate in what others, from Walter Jackson Bate and Francis Gallaway to Meyer Abrams and Peter Otto, have claimed the various romanticisms to have been.

As well, an inevitable concomitant of this approach has been the discovery that, long before Edgar Allan Poe, an author from the American colonies enjoyed, for a significant time, a traceable persuasive moment upon several Europeans, especially Samuel Taylor Coleridge. What must be pointed out, beyond the connections to Coleridge and others, is the simple global direction. Rather than the timeworn notion that, before Poe, ideas crossed the Atlantic exclusively from Europe to the colonies, now we must open our minds to the unmistakable reality that the principles of Wheatley's imagination poetics sailed from the New World to the Old, reversing the conventional wisdom that finds this transatlantic phenomenon to have been virtually impossible.

Acknowledgments

I have been toying for several years with the idea that Wheatley's imagination poetics crossed to the other side of the Pond. Luckily, I have found the time to record this phenomenon. One always serious and informed advisor has been Scot Danforth, director of the University of Tennessee Press, who told me, after reading a draft of this monograph, "Well, I am convinced." It was at that moment that I could finally take pride in my efforts. Other members of the press who have been supportive are Kerry Webb, acquisitions editor; Robert Land, freelance copyeditor; Stan Ivester, managing editor; and Thomas Wells, copyediting assistant.

Many of my colleagues who have encouraged me with this delightful project (I have thoroughly enjoyed every stage which has led to this book) include James A. Levernier, professor of English at the University of Arkansas, who has constantly reinforced my efforts; Zabel Stodola, professor of English at Arkansas; Philip Richards, professor of English at Colgate University; Cheryl A. Elzy, dean of Illinois State University Libraries; Vanetta Mae Schwartz, professor at Milner Library, ISU; and Gary R. Thiel, library assistant at Milner Library. Among those who always make my life easier are Irene Taylor, Angela Scott, Diane Smith, and Jean R. Ballowe.

Kenneth Earl entered several manuscript drafts and prepared the index. Zach Petrea, Jennifer Billingsley, Ken Earl, Andrew Hand, Maureen Anderson, Louis Schroeder, Laurie Brummett, Gary Thiel, and Devona Mallory also offered valuable assistance as they critiqued portions of my argument while listening to me drone on in the classroom.

I should also like to thank Cedric May, professor of English at the University of Texas, Arlington, and the anonymous reader, both of whom read this manuscript for the press and provided generous and constructive criticism.

But my heartfelt gratitude goes to my friend and colleague Russell Rutter, who has constantly advised me, "No John, you aren't unhinged; there is a kind of logic in your findings," and to Alvin Clarence Bowman, president of the Illinois State University, for their steady support.

Chapter 1

Before Wheatley:
The Imagination from Plato to Bruno

The date was February 17, 1600. The place, Rome. As the flames climbed toward Giordano Bruno's defiant frame, the Inquisition had at least to concede that seven years of attempts to coerce the accused's confession or to force his endorsement of Roman Catholic orthodoxy had certainly failed. Among the several heresies with which Bruno was charged was a declaration in his *De magia*, which he repeated in his *De imaginum*, that the human imagination was the mind's supreme faculty. One hundred seventy-three years later, the Early American poet Phillis Wheatley made this declaration when she stated in her *Poems on Various Subjects, Religious and Moral*, printed in London, that the imagination is "the leader of the mental train" (67).*

While Wheatley, America's first African American to publish a book on any subject, was in little danger of being burned at the stake, she assuredly did knowingly risk being labeled a heretic of orthodox literary aesthetics. Indeed, Alexander Pope, whom Wheatley has nauseatingly been accused of slavishly imitating and whose era has been called the Age of Pope, spoke for most British authors when he wrote that "Imagination plies her dang'rous art" (*Essay on Man*, II: 143). What had earlier earned Bruno's violent death would certainly have resulted, had Wheatley been taken seriously, in the public's utter contempt for her entire collection. As a Black woman slave author, Wheatley openly expressed a heresy that, as the following pages demonstrate, helped to revolutionize the world of literary aesthetics.

Prior to an examination of how Wheatley came to shape her revolutionary aesthetics of imagination, we need to touch base with what those authors, from both the ancient world and from the Renaissance, whom Wheatley most likely would have known, had to say regarding the operation of the then

---

*This citation and all subsequent citations to Wheatley's works are taken from the *Collected Works*.

controversial imaginative faculty. Among the ancients with whom Wheatley would have probably been familiar number Plato, Aristotle, Horace, Longinus, and Augustine. Those Renaissance writers whose work she would have seen include Tyndale and his translations of salient passages from the Pentateuch (replicated in such succeeding Bibles as the Coverdale, the Geneva, and the King James versions); Shakespeare, especially his remarks on imagination in *A Midsummer Night's Dream;* and Pierre Charron, whose observations on imagination in his *De la sagesse,* are provocative. Even closer to Wheatley, within her adoptive Boston were the writings of Mather Byles (one of her principal literary mentors), Joseph Seccombe, Samuel Cooper (another mentor), and William Billings (with whom on one occasion Wheatley collaborated). While we deal with Charron, Byles, Seccombe, Cooper, and Billings in the next chapter, now we examine the ancients and Shakespeare—all of whom, ancients and moderns, register concrete connections to Wheatley, either as textual resources or as literary influences.

It should be pointed out that the availability of Latin translations of Plato and Aristotle was fairly broad after 1500 (see Bolgar 173, 278–79, and 434), and Aristotle's *De anima* (an analysis of faculty psychology) in Latin, was widely used as a grammar-school text during the seventeenth and eighteenth centuries in England and in the American colonies. Wheatley's expert knowledge of Latin and her access to several of the largest libraries of her day would surely have brought her into contact with whatever English or Latin texts by Plato or Aristotle she may have wished to consult.

While Plato's strident omission of poets from his ideal *Republic* and his assertion in the *Ion* that poets were mad are and were well known, the intellectuals of Wheatley's time were at least as familiar with Plato's striking metaphor of the charioteer from his *Phaedrus.* In this tract, Plato casts his understanding of the operation of the soul's faculties as a figure divided into three parts: the charioteer, embodying reason (which instructs the will); a black horse, tending toward misrule, representing the appetitive senses, including the imagination; and a white horse representing an extension of the rational faculty, manifested by a properly instructed will. In Plato's vision this rational will is, of course, "a lover of honor and modesty and temperance" or *sophrosyne* (413). What Plato constructs, then, is a picture of the three faculties of the human soul: the memory (comprising the appetites, senses, and imagination), the reason (the rational faculty), and the will (ideally receiving instruction from a species of right reason). Clearly in this schema, that faculty which acts with misrule, coming from the memory alone, fails to manifest the preferred rational behavior. So imagination very early on essentially gets a bad name.

In Aristotle, Plato's two horses "correspond in a figure more nearly to the appetitive and moral or semi-rational soul" (372). According to Aristotle himself, in *On the Soul* (*De anima*), the appetitive portion, coterminous with the imagination, functions as "a movement resulting from an actual exercise of a power of sense" (682). Note that here the imagination moves and exercises in a powerful manner; it is, therefore, to be grasped as a wholly active entity, much as in Plato. And as in Plato, imagination, once again, may lead to mistaken conclusions, as when one "remembers when he really does not"; therefore, we may say that "men follow their imaginations contrary to knowledge" (688). In both Plato and Aristotle, the imagination, which in Aristotle may stimulate "the mind to [a] desired movement" (718), is hardly to be taken as infallible.

Aristotle is perhaps the first to point out that, for human beings, "sight is the most highly developed sense." The name given to imagination, *phantasia* or fancy, has been formed, so says Aristotle, from the Greek *Φάos* or light "because it is not possible to see without light" (682). The word "imagination," of course, derives from the Latin *imago,* picture, likeness, or image. So when we come to Addison's emphasis, in the *Spectator* essays of 1712, upon the eye as principal indicator of an active imagination or fancy that "pictures" to the "eye" (Addison was an expert classicist), we should not be surprised to find that "fancy" and "imagination" are virtually synonyms, and have been for several centuries prior to Addison's analysis. Wheatley inherited this synonymous usage, although she did not continue this tradition.

Perhaps Aristotle's insistence that "without an image thinking is impossible" (714) encouraged, during the seventeenth and eighteenth centuries, usage of the word "thought" as a synonym for both "fancy" and "imagination" (*Oxford English Dictionary*). Hence we may interpret Wheatley's "Thoughts on Being Brought from Africa," a 1768 title for her most frequently anthologized poem, "On Being Brought From Africa," and "Thoughts on the Works of Providence" to be exercises of her imagination. The later "Thoughts on the Times," a contribution to the projected volume of 1779 but never published, may well have manifested yet another exercise in the honing of her aesthetics of imagination.

Of interest to those of us trying to understand Wheatley's experiment in literary aesthetics is Horace's now almost proverbial observation in *Ars poetica* (ca. 18 BC) that, as in painting, so in the poem (*Ut pictura poesis*). Herein we see that image has become particularized as a concrete reference to a painting. Just so Wheatley, who of course could have read Horace's immensely popular *Art of Poetry* in the original Latin, speaks enthusiastically of Scipio Morehead's paintings in "To S.M. a Young African Painter, on Seeing His Works." She declares that Morehead's paintings demonstrate that the artist has translated "thought [imagination] in [to] living characters." Indeed, Morehead, the painter, has combined his talent and his palette to produce "breathing figures" who have "learnt from thee to live" (114).

Extending this investigation of image, Longinus, in his *On the Sublime* (*Peri hupsous*), writing in Greek in the first century, a bit later than Horace, states, in Aristotelian fashion, that "the *image* or *imagination* is applied to every idea of the mind, in whatever form it presents itself, which gives birth to speech." Longinus then notes, "But at the present day the word is predominantly used in cases where carried away by enthusiasm and passion, you think you see what you describe, and you place it before the eyes of your hearers" (91). The implication herein is that once more imagination has become an unreliable, even false faculty.

Longinus, nonetheless, moves on to assert something remarkable and new. Predicting eighteenth-century writers from Akenside to Kant, Longinus records that "our imaginations often pass beyond the bounds of space" (102). In this last statement, Longinus introduces to literary aesthetics the possibility of cosmic flight of imagination and unmistakably identifies the imagination as the agent of this movement of mind. Longinus's *On the Sublime* was virtually unknown in the West from the time of its composition until the first Renaissance edition (in Greek) came out in 1554 (at Basel), but was not popularized until after the great interest stimulated by the 1674 French translation of Nicolas Boileau-Despreaux. In England, William Smith's 1739 English translation enjoyed four reprintings by 1770 and probably encouraged such enthusiastic renderings of the cosmic imagination as Mark Akenside's 1744 *The Pleasures of Imagination,* from which Wheatley borrows the phrase "silken fetters," which appeared in her "On Imagination" and in Akenside's *Pleasures* in book 2, l. 562.

As Wheatley is herself at great pains in her poetry to exceed every boundary of mind, Longinus's provocative observation and any like it she may have encountered would surely have arrested her attention. While we have no real evidence (beyond assertion) that Wheatley knew Greek, she could certainly have come across this striking passage in William Smith's English version of *On the Sublime,* noted above. In stark agreement with Longinus, Wheatley traces in "Thoughts on the Works of Providence" a realm within sleep wherein "ideas range / Licentious and unbounded o'er the plains" (47). The poet has here spoken of boundless regions in whose infinite space, the mind can enjoy even a kind of indulgent profligacy, preparing us for these striking lines from her later "On Imagination": "We on thy [imagination's] pinions can surpass the wind, / And leave the rolling universe behind" (66).

The next major player with whose theoretics of imagination Wheatley was probably familiar was Augustine, bishop of Hippo, whose *De civitate dei* (*City of God*) was so influential on the evolution of the Roman Catholic Church. While the influence of *De trinitate* (*On the Holy Trinity*) on Wheatley may or may not have been direct, Augustine's treatise deals extensively with the imaginative faculty, and analyzes the memory, understanding, and will in terms of God the Father, Son, and Holy Ghost. This analysis later exercised a major role toward defining the essence of the monastic or contemplative life. And *De trinitate* was a necessary text in the curriculum at Harvard College, thereby suggesting the availability of this text to Wheatley. As Augustine's Latin is not particularly difficult, a reader with the linguistic sophistication of Phillis Wheatley would not have found *De trinitate* to have been troubling.

Our concern for *De trinitate* derives from its conversion of the classical philosophical exercise of the *meditatio,* as noted above, into Augustine's image of the Deity whereby memory, understanding, and will (finally as an act of faith in Jesus as the Christ) symbolizes God the Father, Son, and Holy Ghost. This conversion occupies a majority of the space in *De Trinitate* from chapters 9 through 15. In ancient times (implicit in Plato's Charioteer), the *meditatio* referred to an act of the mind (a discipline of sorts) wherein the faculties of memory (containing the subtrinity of appetites, senses, and imagination), the understanding (reason or intellect), and will are summoned into mental operation. As a conscious, philosophical exercise of mind—say, in the case of Cicero (who refers to *meditatio* in such works as *De inventione* et al.)—as an advocate before the courts, Cicero engages the process for eventual public performance, wherein an attorney, philosopher, or poet deploys this exercise as her or his preparation preceding and during the act of creating a text.

Augustine became well acquainted with the practice of *meditatio* during his early adult years when first at Carthage and then at Rome and Milan, he served—before his spiritual conversion to Christianity—as a rhetor. In fact, he would have taught the process, in effect becoming an authority regarding this philosophical discipline of mind. Following his conversion to Christianity, Augustine became concerned that, redolent of Plato and Aristotle, an overdependence on imagination could lead toward false thought. So in *De trinitate,* whose popularity is exceeded only by that of *De civitate dei,* while imagination can, according to Todd Breyfogle, an authority on Augustinian thought, mediate "between sense, perception, and intellectual knowledge through the reproduction and production [of something new] of images" (Fitzgerald 443), for Augustine, more often than not, "imagination's carnal fictions engulf the soul [or mind] in the libidinous cycle of sin" (Fitzgerald 442).

Hence we can draw an almost straight line between *De trinitate* and Bruno's burning at the stake, for what happens to Augustine's interpretation of the meditative process, soon after the early-fifth-century publication of *De trinitate,* is that it becomes appropriated into the monastic life. As such, the *meditatio* functions as a necessary step in the life of the monastic brother leading, ideally, toward mystical contemplation of the Deity. In other words, the practice of the *meditatio* in Augustinian times began to characterize the contemplative life in distinct contraindication to the active life. As such, the *meditatio* helped to shape Roman Catholic orthodoxy. Augustine's influence on the Renaissance perception of imagination as an unreliable—even, at times, evil—faculty, cannot be exaggerated. So when we see Phillis Wheatley celebrate imagination as an inventive and particularly as a supreme faculty, we can now easily grasp the immense challenge that her 1773 "On Imagination" brought into the arena of orthodox literary praxis.

As well, we can now correct the impression Louis L. Martz has given in his award-winning *The Poetry of Meditation: A Study in English Religious Literature of the Seventeenth Century* (1962), whose text remains unaware of Augustine's *De trinitate,* thus leaving the reader to conclude that it was Ignatius Loyola's 1548 *Spiritual Exercises* that ushered in the seventeenth century's preoccupation with meditative poetry. Edward Taylor's having given his ministerial career (in private) to the meditative practice in his two series of *Poetic Meditations* may hence more readily be explained by the fact that Augustine's *De trinitate* was a required text at Harvard College than by the notion that he may have known Loyola's *Exercises* as Martz suggests; indeed, Taylor, the Puritan, was not given to a fondness for recent "Popish" productions.

I have carefully read Louis J. Puhl's translation of *The Spiritual Exercises* made from Loyola's original Spanish, and I find Loyola's analytical investigation of how the imagination functions as an initiator of the meditative process (all in terms of *Ars memorativa*) to be utterly fascinating and thoroughly Augustinian. I, nevertheless, make much of Martz's misleading treatment of meditative poetry, because it invites later scholars such as Barbara Kiefer Lewalski in her *Protestant Poetics and the Seventeenth-Century Religious Lyric* to ignore the fact that *meditatio* originates as a classical exercise of the mind; the fact that memory, understanding, and will correspond to God the Father, Son, and Holy Ghost; and also to ignore the fact that the imagination is the faculty generating the words, images, and tropes that constitute the lyrics she investigates. In the case of Edward Taylor, to whom she gives a chapter, and later Phillis Wheatley, whom she does not mention, for example, she concludes that he "does not actively grapple with his psyche or his art" (Lewalski 391). Without a more thorough knowledge of the intense engagement that Taylor, and later Wheatley, demonstrably makes of his imaginative faculty, Lewalski misses completely the psychomachia (conflict of the soul) within his *Poetic Meditations,* and would doubtless miss such conflict of the soul within Wheatley.

Just as Taylor certainly did know *De trinitate,* so it becomes even more likely that Wheatley would have been directed by her literary mentors, Mather Byles and Samuel Cooper, both Harvard graduates, to Augustine's *De trinitate*. It is obvious surely by this time that Wheatley refused to heed the restrictions Augustine imposed on imagination. For that matter, neither did Wheatley's two mentors; Byles had admitted the operation of his "wild imagination" (which he does later claim requires the temperance of judgment), and Cooper had, without qualification, identified imagination as a "heaven-born maid" (*Pietas* 45).

Significantly, Wheatley's "Thoughts on the Works of Providence" may be read as a full-fledged *meditatio*. Her *meditatio* displays, nonetheless, some substantial classical influences, such as a ten-line invocation to the muse.

Only "Niobe in Distress . . . ," the second of her two epyllia (or short epics), has another invocation of this length. While Milton's initial invocation to *Paradise Lost* runs, by comparison, to a mere four lines, we may conclude immediately that Wheatley is especially concerned with the subject of poetic afflatus. It is clear in this invocation that the condition of her soul or mind (as in Aristotle) is of considerable importance. While her central subject is avowedly "To praise the monarch of the earth and skies" (43), she opens the poem proper with a detailed astronomical description of the earth in relation to the sun and proceeds to emphasize the great "*Pow'r*" and "*Wisdom*" that Providence's works manifest. Then she moves into an exploration of the earth's "face of nature," thereby delving into God's works, which fall much closer to her personal experience. The heavens and the earth, thence, become to her embodiments of God's wisdom, which she chooses to read in God's natural phenomena.

Like Augustine in *De trinitate,* Wheatley searches in "Thoughts" for indications of God's wisdom. But the path each takes proves to be radically dissimilar. Whereas both Augustine and Wheatley use the meditative process to discover knowledge, which leads to wisdom, Augustine insists that true wisdom may be attained only after the faithful commit their wills to love of Christ. Following this commitment, ". . . a trinity is produced by the mind remembering, understanding, and loving itself" (Augustine 190). This trinity of memory, understanding, and loving God closely resembles the overall structure of Dante's *La commedia,* wherein *Inferno* recalls memory; *Purgatorio,* understanding; and *Paradiso,* love of God manifested as an act of mind—that is, of a faithful soul. While I have not been able to ascertain that Wheatley knew Dante, the point here is that Augustine's interpretation of the *meditatio* approached ubiquity during the broad Renaissance.

Augustine's point is that such a "trinity in the mind, is the image of God" (Augustine 191); for in remembering, understanding, and loving "Him by whom it [the mind/soul] was made," the mind "is made wise itself" (Augustine 191). Wheatley's contemplation in "Thoughts" leads her to find "That *Wisdom,* which attends *Jehovah's* ways." For her, this wisdom "Shines most conspicuous in the solar rays" (44). As frequent readers of Wheatley may expect, the citing of the sun's rays takes her, not to a celebration of Christ as culmination of love, but to observations of the "smiling morn," her mother's Aurora (see Shields, *Phillis Wheatley's Poetics of Liberation* 137–38).

Toward the end of "Thoughts," Wheatley appears on the brink of capitulating to Augustinian thought when she dramatizes an exchange between the "mental pow'rs" (48), "*Reason*," and "*Love*," ostensibly evoking Augustine's will as love. Unlike Augustine, whose analysis of love or *caritas* immediately summons up devotion to Christ/God, Wheatley's "Infinite *Love*" functions as "Nature's constant voice" (49), disclosing a universe constructed for "the good of man." Hence Wheatley brings back into view the distinctly human, not as in Augustine the immortal eternality of God, but moving closer to Wordsworth's celebration of nature. Wheatley continues, quite provocatively, to chastise "man ungrateful" toward her idea of God "whose works [are] array'd with mercy." Why mercy? Here Wheatley suggests that proper understanding of God's works should lead the appreciative among humankind to show mercy toward those persons, here but thinly veiled, held in bondage, those such as herself. Having accomplished this gesture of mercy, then, "What song should rise, how constant, how divine" (50).

Wheatley, with her overriding concern for her oppressed Black brothers and sisters (as well as for herself), has apparently found the sort of love advocated by Augustine's "feverish" determination to ascribe all eventualities of this life to a realm of postponed immortality simply insufficient to the present moment. Wheatley's poetic energies, then, as we will see repeatedly in subsequent pages, are brought into the service of attaining freedom, here and now. To be sure, this subtle "mission" (of sorts) remains, however intensely felt, subversive (see Shields, *Phillis Wheatley's Poetics of Liberation* passim). Indeed, earlier in "Thoughts," the poet, once again so very unlike Augustine, gives her attention to "reason's pow'rs" as they function in sleep. "Say, what is sleep?" so the poet asks, "When action ceases, and ideas range / Licentious and unbounded o'er the plains."

At this juncture Wheatley reverses her once cosmic expanse of mind to embrace an individual, personalized, and wholly internal vision regarding the operation of her own mind. Having left behind the external world of wonder, she now enters the equally wonderful realm of her infinite mind. Indeed, herein she can pursue that which is "Licentious," and hear "in soft strains the dreaming lover sigh" or "rave in jealousy." By the time Augustine composed *De trinitate,* he was certainly not himself interested in considering the actions of would-be lovers. Nor does he ever in *De trinitate* take up the subject of absolute freedom of the mind.

Particularly not his concern in *De trinitate,* moreover, is Wheatley's arresting description of sleep as a domain wherein "*Fancy's* queen in giddy triumph reigns" (47). The striking impact of this line to Wheatley's theoretics of imagination can hardly be exaggerated. Fancy clearly occupies in this line a position of subordination to her queen, imagination—for in "On Imagination," Wheatley pointedly names imagination the "imperial queen." This monumental moment in the evolution of her literary aesthetics separates fancy from imagination, placing the former in secondary relation to the latter, suggesting that fancy serves imagination as a species of agent.

Augustine, having no interest in imagination beyond identifying it as a suspicious mediator between the senses and the intellect, registers an essentially negative disposition toward this faculty. We see this perspective regarding the operation of imagination multiple times among others of Wheatley's predecessors. Whereas Augustine intends to explore the meditative process primarily as preparation for (the hope for) mystical contemplation of the Deity, Wheatley wishes to harness the power of her own imagination, which she calculatedly promotes to supreme faculty of her mind. Here she provocatively anticipates Wordsworth's description of the imagination as "Reason in her most exalted mood," that is, as the poet's reason (see the *Prelude*, 14, l. 192, in Stillinger 360).

So in stark contrast to the church father, Wheatley turns the operation of her mind inward, thereby manifesting, not a search for interior union with the Deity, but a quest for knowledge of how her mind may enable her personal search for a space wherein she may reify her intense desire to be free. Such a preoccupation bespeaks a wholly secular orientation in which an individual hopes to use her or his mental resources to discover a full expression of release from life's vicissitudes, such as hostile slavery. In fact, this determination to achieve a modicum of freedom in the here and now travels a straight road toward the romantics. In effect, then, Wheatley has redirected the Christianized meditative process as established by Augustine toward an analysis of the faculties of memory (comprising the subtrinity of appetites, senses, and imagination), understanding, and will, which essentially turns the entire process on its head wherein imagination becomes supreme faculty. Another way of delineating her achievement is to observe that Wheatley leads the theoretics of imagination toward a secular life, hence bringing about an abject rebellion in thought.

Another episode in the West's application of imagination whose telling must not escape our attention occurs within the peculiar English translation (1530) of two passages within the Pentateuch made by William Tyndale.

Tyndale shared the regrettable fate of Bruno for his efforts to translate the *Biblia Sacra Latina* into vernacular English. Indeed, he was in 1536, the year Anne Boleyn lost her head, strangled and then burned at the stake—but not before he had finished and published his English translation of the New Testament (1526) and the Pentateuch.

The significant passages both come from Genesis and suggest particularly negative assessments of how the imagination proves to lead the mind of mankind astray from godly thinking. Genesis 6:5 reads, in Tyndale's rendering: "every imagination of the thoughts of [human beings'] hearts was only evil continually," while the other passage (from 8:21) differs little from the first: "the imagination of man's heart is evil from his youth." Perhaps unexpectedly, both the later popular Geneva Bible (1560) and the translation eventually to become more popular, the authorized King James Version, take the lead from Tyndale and duplicate his translations.

What I find amazing about these two passages is not only the hostility each bears toward the imaginative faculty, but in addition the fact that Tyndale, and subsequently the later two translations, does (do) not attend to Jerome's close paraphrase in his Latin Vulgata, which eventually became sanctified as the *Biblia Sacra*. In his Vulgata, Jerome gives the first passage, which he took from the Hebrew, as: "*Videns Deus et cuncta cogitatio intenta cordis esset ad malum omni tempora*" (and God saw [that] the whole conception of the heart [of mankind] was inclined toward evil all the time), and Genesis 8:21 as "*sensus enim et cogitatio humani cordis in malum prona sunt ab adolescentia sua*" (for the understanding and reasoning of the human heart are inclined toward evil, from his youth).

It should be pointed out that the Hebrew word for "inclination" (impulse or tendency) was *yeçer*, and is the salient word Jerome attempted to give in Latin first as "*intenta*" (6:5) and then as "*prona*" (see *The Interpreter's Bible* [1952] 1: 536–39 and 547 and *New Interpreter's Bible* [1994] 1: 384–94). In both cases, Jerome's Latin may readily be translated as "intention" or "inclination." While Tyndale's "imagination" was retained in the Geneva and King James versions, as stated, Tyndale's "imagination" recurs as well in the Revised Standard Version. But note, nevertheless, that the more recent New International and the New Revised Standard versions finally correct Tyndale's apparently willful error by replacing "imagination" with the assuredly more accurate "inclination." Of course, the poet Phillis Wheatley would most probably have seen the *Biblia Sacra,* which was universally used in the Latin grammar schools, and would therefore have discovered Tyndale's error for herself.

Parishioners, both Anglican and Puritan, who had no Latin, were doubtless left in the dark regarding Tyndale's mistranslation; those without Latin would have tended to swallow hook, line, and sinker William Perkins's diatribe against imagination in his *A Treatise of Man's Imaginations Shewing His Naturall Euill Thoughts: His Want of Good Thoughts: The Way to Reforme Them* (1607). In this tract Perkins, one of the Puritan fathers, admonishes that children (adults, we are left to conclude, should know better) must be dissuaded from depending too much on this suspicious faculty: " . . . the imaginations of man's heart are euill from his youth [from Genesis 8:21], therefore they [i.e. parents, masters, and tutors] must all joyne hand in hand betime to stop up or at least to lessen this corrupt fountain" (164–65).

I find myself unable to resist pointing out that Perkins's "corrupt fountain" reveals just how actively and even creatively this Puritan's imagination has functioned. Perkins further cautions that " . . . the cause of naturall Imagination in them [children], . . . without the special grace of God, will bring eternall condemnation both to souls and bodie" (167). Considering that this warning is being trumpeted a mere seven years after Bruno's sad burning, Perkins's words may be expected to have exercised a dramatic effect, particularly upon those who had no Latin. To be sure, Perkins, a fellow of Christ College, Cambridge, would have been well informed regarding his obvious equivocation.

Unquestionably, Phillis Wheatley subscribed to no such prescription. Unlike Tyndale and his ilk, who must have harbored a powerful distrust of imagination, this distrust became promoted by such later authoritative voices as Hobbes, Locke, and Jonathan Edwards. For that matter, this conservative Christian attitude toward the imaginative faculty has not budged, even down to recent times. This position holds that, in order for the imagination to function "safely," only one who possesses the gift of God's grace can properly display this faculty.

In an article appearing in the ministerial journal *Leadership,* for example, Warren W. Wiersbe remarks in "Imagination: The Preacher's Neglected Ally" (1983), certainly a seductively positive title, that the brand of imagination he extols must be a "sanctified imagination"—disappointingly not so positive. Given the fact that one does not know for certain whether the Deity has bequeathed the gift of grace until after death, how is it, then, that one may ever rely on one's imagination? Without doubt, Wheatley never appears, in the poetry of her two mature periods (see Shields, *Phillis Wheatley's Poetics of Liberation*), willing even to entertain such a delimiting conception for her imagination.

While we are forced to conclude that Tyndale's willful error fostered a considerably negative view of the imaginative faculty, one that was left for the romantics to overcome (was Wheatley a romantic?), William Shakespeare, in his *A Midsummer Night's Dream,* casts an ostensibly positive interpretation upon this mental faculty. As no one of whom I am aware has ever drawn a concrete connection between Shakespeare and Wheatley, the time has come to do so. The text of Shakespeare Wheatley would most likely have known would probably have been Pope's six-volume edition of Shakespeare, owned by Mather Byles.

Others may well discover additional uses of Shakespeare in our widely read poet; to make our point, nevertheless, two traceable adaptations from the great bard suffice at this juncture. In the 1767 "To the University of Cambridge in New England," Wheatley, during the period of her juvenilia, cautions the unruly undergraduates (of Harvard) to eschew sinful behavior, or as she puts it so well, she counsels these youths to "Suppress the deadly serpent in its egg" (16). This most striking metaphor for putting down bad conduct may at first invite a biblical comparison. But checking into a concordance yields no positive clues. Looking into the texts of Shakespeare, however, proves to be much more productive.

In his *Julius Caesar,* Shakespeare has a closely similar passage, whose pertinent three lines read: "And therefore think him as a serpent's egg, / Which, hatch'd, would as his kind grow mischievous, / And kill him in the shell" (2.1.31–33). Here Brutus soliloquizes upon what he deems to be Caesar's "abuse of greatness" (l. 18), which, so he holds, is fast reaching the dangerous dimensions of a tyrant's "mischievous" potential. Wheatley's adaptation redraws the serpent metaphor in a Christian context wherein mischievous behavior becomes an expression of sin, requiring immediate suppression. While viewing human events within a Christian context assuredly does characterize the period of her juvenilia, in her later first and second periods of maturity, a Christian context recurs with far less repetition. In these later times, Wheatley much more often casts her thought within a classical and personally theoretical domain. What is, nevertheless, most interesting about this particular adaptation is the fact that Wheatley, when only about fourteen, has managed to condense Shakespeare's three lines into one.

Wheatley's second adaptation from Shakespeare occurs in the important poem "On Recollection." Asserting that, having attained the age of eighteen, she has watched the vicissitudes of "that period pass," she now, in recollection, discovers "them writ in brass!" (63). In *Henry VIII* (which Shakespeare knew as *All Is True*), Katherine of Aragon, Henry's first wife, and her attendant, Griffith, are lamenting the passing of Cardinal Woolsey (particularly generous of Katherine); this occasion moves Griffith to opine that "Men's evil manners live in brass, their virtues / We write in water" (4.2.45–46). One assumes Griffith is referring to Woolsey's unhappy efforts to petition the pope for an annulment of Katherine's marriage to Henry, so we most immediately tend to view the cardinal's "evil manners" recorded in brass. Wheatley cites only those "manners writ in brass"; in this instance, the Black poet appears to be recognizing the horrible deeds visited upon her and hers by the wretched institution of slavery (see my discussion of this poem in Shields, *Phillis Wheatley's Poetics of Liberation*).

Surely Wheatley's reading of Shakespeare would have brought her to this passage from *A Midsummer Night's Dream,* one of his best known:

> The lunatic, the lover, and the poet
> Are of imagination all compact.
> One sees more devils than vast hell can hold;
> That is the madman. The lover, all as frantic,
> Sees Helen's beauty in a brow of Egypt.
> The poet's eye, in a fine frenzy rolling,
> Doth glance from heaven to earth, from earth to heaven;
> And as imagination bodes forth
> The forms of things unknown, the poet's pen
> Turns them to shapes, and gives to aery nothing
> A local habitation and a name. (5.1.7–18)

Note the repeated enjambment, particularly in the passage describing how imagination shapes the poet's thought. This enjambment alerts the reader that this passage is a particularly intense one. In the "madman" passage we may remember Plato's *Ion;* the "Helen" lines rehearse the mishaps that befall the lovers and fairies in the wood near Athens. The somewhat longer passage devoted to the eye of the poet per se, perhaps equally as excited as in the lines above, though neither unhinged nor misdirected, recalls Aristotle's identification that fancy has its linguistic origin in that which enables vision, light, and as well Augustine's observation on imagination but with a significant caveat. Augustine speaks disparagingly about "things which are not seen" and which become "thought under a fancied image." Such recollections derive from a will seeking earthly pleasure—not from a mind calculated to focus upon the Deity (Augustine 129, 153). Clearly Shakespeare's phrase, "forms of things unknown," departs from Augustine.

The visual imagery sparked in imagination enabling the mind to travel from heaven to earth and earth to heaven begins to sound like Longinus's emphasis on the capacity of imagination to embrace a perception of space, as well as touching base with Bruno's discussion in *De imaginum signorum et ideasum compositione* (1591). As Bruno was in England from the spring of 1583 to October 1585, where he caused quite a stir, especially among the Oxonians, his works, several published in London during his stay, may have provoked the young Shakespeare's curiosity. Bruno spent most of his visit in London, where he closely associated with the Italian ambassador to Elizabeth I's court. Shakespeare himself was apparently in London by 1587 or so, well within the wake of public response to the controversy brought by Bruno's visit.

It is, nevertheless, Bruno's Latin *De imaginum,* wherein he argues that the imagination is the supreme faculty of the human mind—this interpretation of course flying fully in the face of Aristotelian and Augustinian thought— that appears to resonate with the passage quoted above from *A Midsummer Night's Dream.* This "happy" resonance, however, comes into doubt when we take note first of the remainder of the passage quoted and second when we factor in some additional details from the circle encompassing the last years of Bruno's career.

Theseus, Duke of Athens and of course the representative of social order, begins his lengthy speech in which we find the imagination passage, with a response to Hippolyta's reaction to having just heard the rather bizarre claims of Lysander and Demetrius that "'Tis strange, my Theseus, that these lovers speak of." Theseus opens his explanation with this sobering comment: "More strange than true. I never may believe / These antic fables, nor these fairy toys" (5.1.1–3). Consistent with his initially grave attitude, he follows his discourse on imagination with this summative observation: "Such tricks hath strong imagination" (5.1.18). So in Theseus's mind the imaginative faculty manufactures mere "tricks," which we are led to believe must not be taken seriously.

Ignoring the probability that Shakespeare the artist may well be diametrically opposed to this belittling of imagination (how can we know what the dramatist/poet really thought?), we must concede that Shakespeare's character, Theseus, who serves as a representative and even a restorer of order, bespeaks the position of the status quo. As such he would "appear" to side with the public's perception of imagination supposedly taught then by Augustine and the Geneva Bible. As *A Midsummer Night's Dream* did not appear until 1595 and Bruno's *De imaginum* was published in 1591, Shakespeare probably had an opportunity to take a look at this controversial man's certainly controversial work (perhaps his most controversial, for it would seem to have sealed his doom). Even so, Shakespeare proved to be a better survivor than Bruno.

Despite his veneer of conformity, Shakespeare has, perhaps subversively, endorsed, and enthusiastically so, the operation of imagination first by identifying this controversial faculty as the intellectual property of poets and then by noting that this faculty can, in the poet's hands, give substance to "forms" heretofore unknown, hence to his play, a wonderful exercise in the employment of imagination, "A local habitation and a name" (5.1.17). I am tempted to find in Puck's closing words one final effort to dissuade the dramatic poet's audience from concluding that Shakespeare has actually defied custom by calling his new "forms" merely innocuous "shadows," all "but a dream." Wheatley, nevertheless, living in an era more tolerant of controversial ideas (though not so enlightened that it excluded slavery), opted not to allow her own mind to subscribe to imagination as a trick-making faculty.

The point I am trying to make here is not that the above discourse must be taken as a hard interpretation of Shakespeare's play, but that Wheatley herself may well have taken the bard's presentation of how the imagination functions to a poet, perhaps to any poet, as a subversive celebration of imagination. Indeed, this probability of how she may have understood Theseus's take on imagination is certainly compatible to Wheatley's own celebration in "On Imagination." If the Black poet viewed Shakespeare's observations as an exercise in subversion—a creative approach to composition which, during her first period of maturity, had great appeal for her—then his discourse on imagination may have had a most positive impact on her quest for personal release from a hostile world.

As we have observed, adumbrations of Plato, Aristotle, Horace, Longinus, Augustine, and Tyndale may be traced in Shakespeare's fecund treatment of imagination in *A Midsummer Night's Dream*. When so read, Shakespeare's remarks help to prepare us for the journey toward Wheatley's revolutionary theoretics of imagination. It is also pertinent to note that Samuel Taylor Coleridge, as a grammar school student, was exposed to heavy doses of Shakespeare. So we see that both Wheatley and Coleridge became intimately familiar with the great bard at parallel moments in their individual development.

Chapter 2

Before Wheatley: The Imagination from Bruno to William Billings

As our investigation of Wheatley's pursuit of knowledge regarding her forebears' understanding of the imaginative faculty continues, we now concentrate on how thinkers and writers whom Wheatley may have consulted and those she actually did consult analyzed imagination after Bruno's martyrdom. Just to clear the air about Wheatley's alleged slavish imitation of Alexander Pope, particularly regarding his position on imagination, we preface our consideration of the French Charron, other British writers, and the named Early American contemporaries of Wheatley with a brief excursus examining the weight of actual evidence detailing this alleged influence.

Almost certainly, Wheatley would have become familiar with Pope's *Works* by way of Mather Byles, Wheatley's principal literary mentor, who lived across the street from the Wheatley mansion. This same Byles, named for his uncle, Cotton Mather, inherited the majority of his uncle's extensive library upon his death in 1728. According to Peter T. Kyper, Byles's library contained "over two thousand volumes" and "was considered one of the best in the colonies." Kyper is careful to add that, because of Byles's strong literary leanings, his library housed "a great number of literary works (as opposed to theological works)" (Kyper 3). As Kyper claims that Byles very likely owned a copy of Pope's *Works* by the late 1730s, Wheatley would have had easy access to Pope's printed poems and "Prefaces."

In his usually helpful *The Creative Imagination: Enlightenment to Romanticism,* James Engell records that Pope refers to imagination only once in the early *Essay on Criticism* (1711) but notes in the "Preface" to his translation of Homer's *Iliad* (1715) that Homer projects a peculiar "Force of the poet's Imagination" (40). While this early description strikes an almost enthusiastic chord, reflecting, so Engell holds, exposure to Addison's positive evaluation of imagination, in his 1712 *Spectator* series of essays devoted to explanation of "the pleasures of the imagination," clearly by publication of the second epistle of *An Essay on Man,* appearing in March 1733, Pope has rethought his earlier, positive position toward the imaginative faculty. Indeed, here "Imagination plies her dang'rous art / And pours it [what fills the head] all upon the peccant part" (Pope 134). Significantly Engell fails to point out this shift in Pope's judgment, although, given the availability of Pope's texts to her, Phillis Wheatley surely did not fail to come across this shift.

If Wheatley is supposed to have placed so much store on Pope's works and thought, then why does she, in her crucial "On Imagination," celebrate imagination, particularly the operation of her own, with undeniable vim and verve? For response to this query we must, perhaps surprisingly, travel no further than the writers of Wheatley's eighteenth-century New England. It is ironic that the orthodox Joseph Sewall, son of the diarist Samuel Sewall and Wheatley's religious "monitor," according to her own testimony, served as a conduit to the early-sixteenth-century skeptic, Pierre Charron.

Charron, a friend and later a disciple of Michel de Montaigne, published in 1601, within a year of Bruno's burning, his famous *De la sagesse,* which includes a lengthy and detailed investigation of how the imagination functions within the human mind. Resonating with Shakespeare's enthusiastic description, Charron focuses on imagination as a powerful faculty of the mind, second only to the understanding. He also does something quite unexpected; he subordinates, for a brief moment, fancy to imagination.

The connection to Charron that Joseph Sewall enabled for Phillis Wheatley was bridged by Joseph Seccombe, who has the distinction of authoring the first tract on sport published in America, a sermon extolling the value of fishing, especially on the Sabbath. Sewall had delivered Seccombe's ordination sermon, in which Seccombe and two other young clergy were commissioned to minister to Native Americans. After three years of service, which clergy in New England and Britain judged to have been distinguished, Seccombe accepted a call to the church at Kingston, New Hampshire. He assumed the duties of minister in October 1737, after which Seccombe settled down (having married in January 1738) to the relatively quiet life of a prosperous parson.

Seccombe was not always well fixed, however; having humble origins, Joseph found himself, because of his evident intelligence and genteel disposition, well supported in his grammar school days and throughout his college tenure at Harvard (A.B., 1731). This financial support came from the generosity of Old South Church, which he had joined, following his mother, in 1723. As his ties with Old South Church were, then, almost from the beginning quite strong, and all his publications appeared first in Boston, it is reasonably certain that this thinking man's works were available to the young and eager student, Phillis Wheatley, in the large book repository within Old South Church. Seccombe died in 1760, just a year before Wheatley arrived in Boston. Given Sewall's role as spiritual counselor to Wheatley and his association with Seccombe, Sewall likely directed Wheatley's attention to this man's well-known works.

Perhaps the most substantial link between Wheatley and Seccombe occurs in the several textual connections between Wheatley's last extant poem, "Elegy on Leaving ——," wherein she bides adieu to her poetic pursuits, and Seccombe's "Ye Happy Fields," in which he expresses great reluctance upon leaving behind pristine nature's "sweet Composers of the pensive soul." Seccombe's eight-line poem—which appends his homily, *Business and Diversion . . . in the Fishing Season,* the entire text of which, as we have observed, serves as an apology for the sport of fishing—reads as follows:

> Ye happy Fields, unknown to noise and strife,
> The kind Rewarders of industrious Life;
> Ye shady Woods where once I us'd to rove,
> To think for Man, and praise the God above;
> Ye murmuring Streams that in Meander roll,
> The sweet Composer of the pensive soul,
> Farewell.—The city calls me from your Bowers;
> Farwell amusing Tho'ts and peaceful Hours. (22)

Seccombe's 1734 homily, which was published in Boston and would have been readily available to Wheatley, had in his closing "prayer" on the page preceding "Ye Happy Fields" extolled the "Fields and Groves," "the flowry Beauties" of the warmer seasons (spring, summer, and fall) and the other "Delights" of nature, all redolent of Vergilian pastoral. The minister is studious to explain, in the sermon, nonetheless, that all these "rich Provision[s] of Nature" cannot finally "satisfy . . . the Soul of a Christian." Note, nevertheless, that "Ye Happy Fields" surprisingly contains little, if any, Christianity; rather

Seccombe's poem, unlike the sermon, represents a largely secular vision, as does Wheatley's "Elegy on Leaving ——."

Just as Wheatley describes in her poem, "ye friendly bow'rs," wherein she "pensively... stray'd," and a "pebbl'd brook" which contributes to the ambience of "simple Nature's various charms," all these captivating enchantments of an escape from the "crowds and noise" of an urban setting (156), Seccombe has "shady Woods," "happy Fields," and "murmuring Streams" within which the poet/minister "us'd to rove" to compose his "pensive soul," these enticements resembling Wheatley's phrases depicting refuge from the city's "Noise and Strife." Whereas Wheatley's use of nature bespeaks that of a poet seeking to create poetry, "Rapt with the melody of Cynthio's [the Sun's] strain / There first my bosom felt poetic flame" (156), Seccombe appears disposed to discover the pleasures of nature "To think for Man, and praise the God above," or perhaps to concentrate upon the composition, not of poetry, but of a minister's sermon.

In any event, both Wheatley and Seccombe clearly enjoin a nostalgic world of pastoral and then express definite regret for what each perceives to be a necessary abandonment of this happy, preferred realm. While Seccombe bids "Farewell to amusing Tho'ts [imagination] and peaceful Hours," perhaps so that he can more concentratedly embrace the onus of his ministry, Wheatley, with more at stake, surrenders the writing of poetry, her life's work. She does so, very likely, because of failing health. The thought and images advanced in each writers' poem, nevertheless, indicate more than casual literary parallels.

When we examine another of his sermons, however, we discover that Seccombe may not have been as "safe" a writer as Sewall probably thought him to be. In his ostensibly homiletic, but actually treatise-like *Some Occasional Thoughts* (1742), for example, we encounter the name of the famous skeptic, Pierre Charron, and a quote in a footnote from his *De la sagesse* (*Of Wisdom*). According to Eugene F. Rice Jr., in his *The Renaissance Idea of Wisdom*, Charron's *De la sagesse* (1601) marks "the triumph of wisdom as a naturally acquired moral virtue"—not a gift of God's grace (179). In other words, in this widely circulated Renaissance work, Charron constructed "a purely human wisdom" (179), recalling the ancient, classical understanding of the term. Seccombe's subject in *Some Occasional Thoughts* is the recent spate of enthusiasm brought on by George Whitefield's emotional preaching; Whitefield, about whom Wheatley would later write an internationally published and famous elegy, was chaplain to Selina Hastings, Countess of Huntingdon, who financially backed Wheatley's *Poems,* but was also much hailed as the dramatic "Voice" of the Great Awakening. Even Jonathan Edwards, spearhead of the Great Awakening, had lamented that Whitefield's provocation of trances, visions, and such enthusiastic responses had too often become manifestations of hypocrisy.

As Seccombe opens *Some Occasional Thoughts* with a quote from Edwards, one would expect these two to be in accord. Such is certainly *not* the case. Whereas Edwards in his *Treatise on the Religious Affections* holds firmly that the imagination is the means through which Satan invades the human soul, Seccombe argues that "The Divine Spirit, striving with Man, would operate on the *Imagination.*" Even though Seccombe acknowledges that the imagination is "a lower Power of human Nature" (Wheatley later elevates imagination to the highest level of the mind), he declares that, "Yet under Conduct of Understanding, it's a very useful and powerful Faculty" (*Some Occasional Thoughts* 9).

What provokes further interest here is that, in a footnote to this same passage, Seccombe quotes the following from Charron's *De la sagesse:*

> "Imagination . . . is a loud, a blustering and restless Faculty [which] seems perfectly bound up in the profoundest Sleep, but is continually buzzing at the brain, like a boiling Pot."
> (*Some Occasional Thoughts* 9)

What we notice here is that, although Seccombe appears to cite Charron as an authority on imagination, what he has actually done amounts to an extension of Charron's thought in the passage quoted, in which he somewhat elevates imagination by giving it more favorable press than even Charron had ventured. We find here that Seccombe is assuredly opposed to Edwards's vilification of imagination. Seccombe concludes his discussion of imagination by maintaining, "Though the Divine Spirit makes Use of the Imagination, it can never be serviceable without the Understanding" (9). Observe that Seccombe does not, as Edwards does, insist that imagination can only be trusted if applied by one whose soul has received sanctification.

So although we have not moved to the position to which Wheatley later came, we have certainly departed from Edwards's Calvinistic point of view.

It is worth noting that Seccombe quotes Charron from George Stanhope's 1707 translation of Charron's French *sagesse,* not from the much earlier 1625 Samson Leonard translation, thereby ascertaining that Charron was, in a recast translation, alive and well in Massachusetts Bay; as well, when Seccombe died, he left a library of five hundred volumes. So the copy of *Concerning Wisdom* Seccombe used could well have been his own and thereby have come into the hands of Phillis Wheatley. Seccombe's attitude toward imagination, then, becomes a suitable "theoretical" framework for Samuel Cooper's 1761 positive assertion that "Imagination! [is a] heav'n-born maid" (*Pietas* 45).

Charron, in the Stanhope translation, makes several additional and provocative observations regarding the imaginative faculty, which move beyond Seccombe's interest but which accord provocatively with Wheatley's later theoretics. According to Charron, the imagination is an essential and highly charged faculty that "keeps all [the other parts of the mind] about it awake and sets the other Faculties on *work*" (*Of Wisdom* [trans. Stanhope] 119). Gendering imagination as female, which, given Wheatley's preoccupation with the Muses and with female deities, would have appealed to her, the French skeptic imparts to the feminine faculty great power and responsibility:

> ... the Acts of Recollection, representing to the Intellectual Faculty, laying up in the Memory, and drawing out those Stores again for Use, are all of them Operations of the Imaginative Faculty. (119)

Wheatley's own "On Recollection" speaks of the memory in similar terms as that mental power whose "secret stores ... to the high-raptur'd poet gives her aid" (62).

Most significantly, moreover, Charron maintains further that memory and "Fancy, come within the compass of This [imagination], and are not (as some pretend) Powers of the Mind, distinct and separate from it" (*Of Wisdom* [trans. Stanhope] 119–20). So we observe that, to this important aesthetic theorist, both fancy and memory serve the imagination and are therefore subordinate to it. I have been unable to discover another theorist who insists upon this actually quite specific description of the operation of imagination, until of course we come to Phillis Wheatley. It may be then that this authoritative theorist may well have served Wheatley in a pivotal capacity.

Charron exuberantly holds that the imagination "is *Hot*," which causes poets to indulge "in bold and lofty Flights of Fancy" (Stanhope trans. 116). Here we view a powerful, influential theorist asserting that imagination is clearly associated, as in Wheatley, with the condition of high rapture or intense enthusiasm and with the notion of apparently boundless flight, this last notion echoing Longinus and predicting Akenside's *Pleasures of Imagination*. No less a figure than Francis Bacon in 1605 appears to have taken instruction from Charron when the British philosopher describes imagination as an "extremely licensed" mental power, which can "make unlawful matches and divorses of things" (Bacon 5). Both these thinkers point directly to Wheatley's "Thoughts," wherein she speaks of a realm residing in the dreaming mind where "ideas range / Licentious and unbounded" and "Where *Fancy's* queen in giddy triumph reigns" (47).

To suggest that the New England intelligentsia were unaware of aesthetic thought in Great Britain during the eighteenth century would indeed be preposterous. So, as promised above, we will, in attempting to establish an adequate context for Wheatley's maturing aesthetic theoretics as touches the imagination, journey for a time, among several British thinkers, all of whom would surely have been aware of Charron's *De la sagesse*.

Virtually none of the eighteenth-century British aestheticists, however, pick up on Charron's effort to distinguish imagination and fancy, although they appear to agree with Charron, and many others from Plato and Aristotle to Shakespeare, that the imagination is the poet's faculty. Beyond his somewhat disparaging remarks regarding imagination in *Leviathan,* however, Hobbes, in his 1650 "Answer to Davenant's Preface to *Gondibert,*" makes no distinction between fancy and imagination, genders fancy as a feminine principle, identifies fancy as a faculty of flight which can "fly from one Indies to the other, and from Heaven to Earth," echoing Shakespeare (Hobbes, "Answer" 59), and notes that "Poets are Painters" (61—this last observation recalling Horace). John Dryden, just fourteen years later, puts on the breaks regarding the imagination when he admonishes that "imagination in a poet is a faculty so wild and lawless, that like a high-ranging spaniel, it must have clogs tied to it, lest it outrun judgement" (Engell 35).

Mather Byles, one of Wheatley's mentors who wrote in America almost eighty years later, appears for a time to indulge his "wild imagination" with impunity, as Wheatley would do over a hundred years after Dryden. To return to Britain, John Dennis, called by some the greatest critic of his age, in remarkable disagreement with Locke, celebrates the enthusiastic passions. In the fourth chapter of *The Grounds of Criticism* (1704), entitled "What the Greate Poetry Is, What Enthusiasm Is," Dennis identifies the "Enthusiastick Passions" as "those emotions which excite great poetry. Contemplation and meditation give rise to these emotions" (338), the strongest of which "must be rais'd by religious Ideas; that is, by Ideas which either shew the Attributes of the Divinity, or relate to his worship" (339). In his *Religious Sublime,* David Morris interprets Dennis's perspective as having moved a significant step beyond Longinus. In Morris's words, "For Longinus, the interaction of passion and imagination contributed to the sublime; for Dennis it created the sublime" (66).

Anthony Ashley Cooper, a contemporary of Dennis who was the Third Earl of Shaftsbury and who, according to Douglas Den Uyl, author of the contemporary "Foreword" to Shaftsbury's *Characteristics,* "wrote one of the most important and influential books of the eighteenth century" (A. Cooper 1: vii), remarks in a 1708 "Letter Concerning Enthusiasm" that, regarding poetic afflatus, "*Inspiration* may be justly call'd *Divine ENTHUSIASM:* For the Word itself signifies *Divine Presence,* and was made use of . . . to express whatever was sublime in human Passions" (A. Cooper 1: 34). Perhaps Wheatley actually saw this tract; it is certain that her enthusiastic pursuit of poetic afflatus constitutes a dominant pattern in her poetry.

Sounding much like a paraphrase of Charron, Shaftsbury holds that appetites and desires reside in the imagination, that the imaginative faculty is "a Business which can never stand still" (A. Cooper 1: 199), and that this faculty becomes manifested in "*Giddiness* and *Dream*" (1: 201). Shaftsbury even goes so far as to recommend writing as an invaluable "*self-examining* Practice and Method of *inward* Colloquy" (1: 202). To be sure, here Shaftsbury draws on the introspective tradition of meditation, a tradition that Wheatley clearly inherited. But like Dryden, Shaftsbury strongly advises that fancy (not here made distinct from imagination) and enthusiasm require "some Controuler or Manager" (1: 198); in order to guard against "mere Imagination or the Exorbitancy of Fancy" (2: 90), one must acknowledge that what he insists on here is a healthy moderation, summoning up the classical Greek cultural ideal of *sophrosyne*—nothing in excess, sanity in all things, the golden mean.

While Shaftsbury's sentiments on inspiration could have provided Wheatley useful instruction, Dennis's welding of imagination and the feeling of the sublime of course predicts Wheatley's combination of these two aesthetic categories in "On Imagination." Her work, nevertheless, demonstrates that, once again, she did not agree with Shaftsbury's notion requiring a manager for imagination, or for that matter for the sublime. Indeed, the principle of order in her liberated poetics was the imagination itself. Joseph Addison, Edmund Burke, and Henry Home, Lord Kames, proved to be more favorable, more compatible theorists regarding imagination, and therefore more in line with Wheatley's interpretation than Shaftsbury, although these later British thinkers indicate contiguities of thought no more remarkable than the parallels between the African American poet and the French Charron or the British Dennis.

Joseph Addison, who was one of the most enthusiastic early advocates for imagination and whose *Spectator* was the most widely read of the gentleman's magazines of eighteenth-century England, expressed in language designed to edify English gentlemen some of the most lofty but clearly stated ideas about the sublime working in concert with the imagination. In *Spectator* 412, for example, he writes:

> Our imagination loves to be filled with an Object, or to
> grasp at anything that is too big for its Capacity. We are
> flung into a pleasing Astonishment at such unbounded
> Views, and feel a delightful Stillness and Amazement in
> the Soul at the Apprehension of them. (3: 540)

This passage identifies the imagination as the faculty of one who desires intensely to grasp the infinite and the ineffable. Samuel Holt Monk, author of the authoritative *The Sublime,* holds that what Addison describes here is "essentially the sublime experience from Addison to Kant" (*Sublime* 58).

Wheatley's "On Imagination" articulates the power Addison extols, but with a significant difference:

> From star to star the mental optics rove,
> Measure the skies, and range the realms above,
> There in one view we grasp the mighty whole,
> Or with new worlds amaze the unbounded soul. (30)

Wheatley's words, "view," "grasp," "amaze," "unbounded," and "soul," echo Addison. Like Addison, Wheatley specifies a limitless vision, but she adds the idea of "new worlds." While Addison's description speaks of views in created nature, Wheatley's "new worlds" introduces the poet's conception of myth making. Indeed, Wheatley proceeds to build not one but two heterocosmic worlds in this poem in remarkable anticipation of the apocalyptic romantics.

In his extremely popular *Philosophical Enquiry into the Origin of Our Ideas of the Sublime and Beautiful* (1757), Edmund Burke concentrates on a sensationalist view (which holds that all knowledge originates in sensation) regarding the psychology of the imagination/sublime. Sounding a perception of divine wisdom that parallels Wheatley's, Burke declares,

> Whenever the wisdom of our Creator intended that we should be affected with anything, he did not confide the execution of his design to the languid and precarious operation of our reason; but he endued it with powers and properties that prevent [precede] the understanding, and even the will, which seizing upon the senses and imagination, captivate the soul before the understanding is ready either to join with them or to oppose them. (107)

As we may expect from a psychology of sensation, Burke's center of interest here is directed not toward God and devotion but toward an analysis of response. In Wheatley's work, she, too, is driven to an analysis of how the power of imagination and its attendants—memory, fancy, the senses, and the appetites—interplay in her construction of a poetic world. To be sure, such an undertaking, the creation of a new world, flies fully in the face of Burke's position that "the imagination is incapable of producing anything absolutely new" (Burke 17).

In Wheatley's analysis, however, these powers usurp reason at that moment that she, in remarkable contrast to the Burkean notion of false consciousness, elevates the imagination, having finally absorbed all its attendant parts, to the position of reason as "leader of the mental train" or, indeed, as the poet's "reason." In "On Imagination," then, the poet pictures the mind's eye—that is, the fancy—as seizing upon "some lov'd object" which "all the senses bind, / And soft captivity involves the mind" (65). But in her determination to carve out an idea of infinite space, she opts to ascribe to the unbounded and even at selected moments "licentious" imagination the power(s) of enabling her to launch offensives into the infinite realm of freedom, thereby bypassing the less free, less licensed, understanding or reason.

As Phillis Wheatley was certainly, if regrettably, no stranger to pain and this world's vicissitudes, she may well have found Burke's aesthetic analysis of pain in the *Enquiry* to be useful to her own management of pain, especially in her poetry. Burke affirms, for perhaps the first time, that terror and imagined pain leading to astonishment serve as sources for the idea of the sublime. In anticipation of Kant's "Analytic of the Sublime," as well as Keats's oxymoronic figures of "sad joy," Burke bases his theory of the sublime upon

> Whatever is fitted in any sort to excite the ideas of pain, and danger, that is to say, whatever is in any sort terrible, or is conversant about terrible objects, or operates in a manner analogous to terror. (39)

Monk states that "... in introducing pain as the basis of sublimity, he [Burke] opens the way for the inclusion of ideas and images in art that had hitherto been considered as lying outside the sphere of aesthetic pleasure" (*Sublime* 91). Wheatley derives the emotions of pain and danger that evoke the sublime from three sources within her own experience: first, from the desire to escape temporal "woes, a painful endless train" (152); second, from depicting the wrath of an angry god as in "Goliath of Gath," "Isaiah lxiii," and "Niobe in Distress..."; and third, from an aching reluctance to surrender her poetic world. Despite all these positive correlations between Burke and Wheatley, we must observe that Wheatley did not share Burke's notion wherein imagination brings on false consciousness.

Henry Home, Lord Kames, in his *Elements of Criticism* (1762), focuses, not on pain, but on the pleasure obtainable from imaginative literature. Having settled on Addison's earlier description of grandeur or greatness as the sublime, Kames asserts that the enthusiastic passions "commonly signify the quality or circumstance in objects by which the emotions of grandeur and sublimity are produced; sometimes the emotions themselves" (1: 211). In this last phrase

Kames foreshadows Kant, who will later insist that the sublime does not reside "in any of the things of nature, but only in our own mind" (Kant, *Critique* 114). To Kant, the feeling of the sublime never occurs "in objects" but always results from a mental response to their contemplation. Like Kant, Wheatley, as we have seen, considers the sublime to be a mental response and thereby avoids Lord Kames's tendency to confuse object and response.

In his examination of the sublime, Kames emphasizes height, but he studiously avoids identifying the sublime as an elevated distance above the contemplating person. He does, nevertheless, maintain that "Ascent is pleasant because it elevates us" (1: 220) and that "an expression or sentiment that raises the mind" is "great or elevated" (1: 223). "The effect of motion and force *in conjunction* provokes the most sublime response, which," continues Kames, "the image of the planetary system most successfully stimulates" (emphasis added). In close anticipation of Wheatley's descriptions, Kames even goes so far as to declare,

> But if we could comprehend the whole system at one view,
> the activity and irresistible force of these immediate bodies
> would fill us with amazement: nature cannot furnish
> another scene so grand. (1: 256)

Three lines from Wheatley's "Thoughts on the Works of Providence" amply display Kames's motion combined with force:

> Ador'd the God that whirls surrounding spheres,
> Which first ordain'd that mighty Sol should reign
> The peerless monarch of th' ethereal train. (43)

As we have observed of "On Imagination," the poet and her readers "comprehend the whole system at one view." The mind's eye takes in this view while enjoying the celestial motion:

> From star to star the mental optics rove,
> Measure the skies, and range the realms above,
> There in one view we grasp the mighty whole. (66)

The similarities here are striking. Clearly Wheatley registers proximity of thought with all the British thinkers treated above. At the same time, however, she departs from them when she elevates imagination to the poet's reason and when she constructs new worlds.

Just at a moment when British aesthetic theory would appear to have been warming to Wheatley's use of imagination and the sublime, a reactionary response is levied. In *The Creative Imagination,* James Engell misses this reactionary response when he remarks of William Duff's 1767 *Essay on Original Genius* that Duff "attains a view of the imagination as a broad and natural power whose scope in poetry is 'absolute and unconfined'" (84). Three years after the *Essay,* however, Duff countermands his earlier position. Indeed, in the 1770 *Critical Observations on the Writings of the Most Celebrated Original Geniuses in Poetry,* which Engell does not mention, Duff, toward the end of this later work, finds in the poetry of the Italian Ludovico Ariosto, especially in his *Orlando Furioso,* abundant evidence that, characteristic of original genius, is "an irregular greatness, wildness, and enthusiasm of imagination" (296–97). Duff's radical shift to a decidedly negative position toward the imagination assuredly comes as a surprise in the last pages of *Critical Observations* when he admonishes that "There is indeed at the same time great danger of being betrayed into error, from the unrestrained indulgence of imagination on religious subjects" (353).

If it is true that all great geniuses of letters pursue a nondenominational theology in their work, a process that Wheatley, somewhat following the example of Charron, most assuredly does embrace, then all literary geniuses must err, according to Duff, with stubborn alarm. As for Wheatley's experimentation with heterocosms, Duff maintains that "This tendency to contrive visionary schemes, it is obvious, arises from imagination irregular and unchastised" (*Critical Observations* 356). Such a dangerous imagination must be tamed "by the chastening power of the reasoning faculty" (356). So Duff's final pronouncement against imagination has moved, most disappointingly, not a dust mot away from the position of Jonathan Edwards.

While the British aesthetes at several points appear to be providing Wheatley useful instruction in her intellectual shaping of her own poetics, they finally give her less than courageous or liberal assistance. For the most formative sources of what we may now call Wheatley's rebellious spirit within the realm of literary aesthetics, an aesthetics that clearly points toward romanticism, we must turn, perhaps surprisingly, to Colonial Americans. All these potential teachers resided in Wheatley's own Boston, among whom numbered Joseph Seccombe, Charles Chauncy, some of the poets of the 1761 *Pietas et Gratulatio* (including Samuel Cooper), William Billings, and her principal literary model, Mather Byles.

In his attempt to construct an intellectual history of the imagination in his *Creative Imagination,* James Engell not only neglects to investigate the contribution of Charron's *De la sagesse* or William Duff's *Critical Observations;* he fails to give any attention to Seccombe, Cooper, Chauncy, Billings, or Byles. While he suggests that Philip Freneau initiates an analytical examination of the fancy in "The Power of Fancy" (1770; it is unlikely that Wheatley knew this poem, at least not before her 1773 *Poems*), he finds that no really penetrating pursuit of the imaginative faculty occurred in America before Poe and Emerson (Engell 188–96). I would be remiss if I did not point out that Engell is hardly alone in his failure to recognize a hearty and wholly active appreciation of literary aesthetics among American authors of the eighteenth century. While noting somewhat anemic "intimations of aesthetic sensibility" in the works of Jonathan Edwards, Benjamin Franklin, Thomas Jefferson (for me, a distasteful ascription), and Philip Freneau, for example, Max I. Baym in *A History of Literary Aesthetics in America* makes no mention of the several authors I have cited; conspicuously absent is Phillis Wheatley. As well, in his recent *The Oxford Handbook of Early American Literature,* Kevin J. Hayes, editor, introduces this essay collection by quoting with approval Moses Coit Tyler's jaded notion that "'Undoubtedly literature for its own sake was not much thought of, or lived for, in those days'" (10). I center on Engell's *Creative Imagination,* not to devalue his considerable achievement, but to take advantage of his invaluable tracing of the imaginative faculty, at least as far as his exercise takes him.

Much of the aim of this present monograph is given over to an attempt to initiate correction of the incomplete portrait of Early American aesthetics which Tyler, Hayes, Engell, Baym, and others convey. Exploring such Early American authors as Joseph Seccombe, Mather Byles, and Samuel Cooper, all of whom treat the realm of the imaginative faculty and who were well known to Wheatley, will, I trust, move toward correcting this unfortunate lapse in Early American literary aesthetics.

Joseph Seccombe, Wheatley's fellow traveler on the path toward wisdom, who cited Charron in the Stanhope translation of *De la sagesse,* and Charles

Chauncy, who signed Wheatley's "To the Public"—her letter of attestation regarding the authenticity of her authorship—each commented on the imagination and enthusiasm prompted by the voice of the Great Awakening, George Whitefield. We have already examined Seccombe's endorsement of the imagination. Chauncy, however, despite his identity as an Old Light liberal minister, expressed an opposing attitude toward imagination. For in the same year (1742) as Seccombe's endorsement, Chauncy, in *Enthusiasm Described and Caution'd Against,* declares in rhetoric predicting the hostility that Edwards would show in the later *Affections,* that his purpose in this published sermon is to admonish the people "against the wilds of a heated imagination" (i).

Equating the terms "enthusiasm" and "imagination" throughout this sermon, Chauncy claims with an exaggeration betraying the passion of his own imagination, "*Enthusiastic wildness has slain its thousands*" (iii, emphasis in original). At one point Chauncy even calls imagination "meer [*sic*] pretense" (2). Despite the fact that he acknowledges that the etymology of imagination "carries in it a good meaning, as signifying inspiration from God" (3), he stubbornly insists, "But the word is more commonly used in a bad sense, as intending an *imaginary,* not a *real* inspiration" (3). Toward the sermon's end, Chauncy holds "Next to the Scripture, there is no greater enemy to *enthusiasm,* than *reason*" (18). This last remark reawakens Augustine.

Here this minister displays the conservative position of a New Light Calvinist, a contradictory posture for one whose career has been judged to have been that of a liberal. Chauncy's assertions are, nevertheless, the more interesting for two reasons. First, if he is to be believed, that imagination is "more commonly used in a bad sense," then Seccombe's position toward this faculty assumes the character of rebellion. Second, Chauncy's equation of imagination and the enthusiastic passions or the feeling of the sublime only reinforces the argument that, by 1742 in Wheatley's Boston, these two aesthetic categories were thought to blend or to operate inseparably. Although Chauncy held that the operation of these two faculties in concert could only lead to perdition (in accord with Edwards's *Affections*), Seccombe assuredly did not; in his opinion, the path from imagination to the divine is direct and unobstructed. As well, of course, all this attention given to the imagination/sublime attests irrefutably that this faculty enjoyed considerable public impact, hence negativity underscoring Engell's ignorance regarding Early Americans' growing aesthetic sophistication. This contextualization of Wheatley's later experimentation with imagination can only raise our expectations that her experiment was not only credible but may well have been, given her obvious predilection for aesthetics, inevitable.

Samuel Cooper (1725–1783), who was old enough to have read these tracts by Seccombe and Chauncy when published, demonstrates in the thirteenth poem of the 1761 *Pietas et Gratulatio,* ostensibly a celebration of the accession of George III, that he has not merely agreed with Seccombe, but that he has extended the earlier minister's analysis of imagination. In the first of the two English poems in *Pietas,* the thirteenth and the twenty-eighth, thought by the most reliable authorities to be by Cooper (Akers, *Divine* 376–77n40), the poet repeats his intense desire for liberty so evident in the "dedicatory" essay. For example, Cooper disperses throughout this elegy on George II's death such phrases as "liberty, bright goddess," "every patriot [with] virtue crown'd" and a "grand design.... Sacred to liberty and law" (*Pietas* 46, 47). Cooper closes the poem with an image of the new young monarch, George III, "Stretching each nerve to freedom's goal.... For Heaven and Earth delight in Patriot Kings" (*Pietas* 51–52). The language here closely resembles that of Wheatley, especially in "To George Washington" and "Liberty and Peace."

In the following stanza lamenting the death of George II, however, Cooper states his full grasp of imagination as an aesthetic category:

> Imagination! Heaven-born maid!
> Descend and dissipate the cloud,
> The black'ning cloud, which soils the mind
> Too deeply tinctur'd with its grief:
> Oh! Speak the virtues of the godlike man. (*Pietas* 45)

Without qualification (no necessary manager, as in Shaftsbury et al.), Cooper identifies imagination as the divine maiden, Minerva or Athena, personification of wisdom. In this stanza, imagination does not merely work in association with the divine; she is herself divine and is asked to descend from her sublime abode to "dissipate" Cooper's "black'ning cloud" of grief by speaking or narrating the deceased's accomplishment.

With this poem, Phillis Wheatley, as a student of poesis, may well have been guided by her "Friend [Cooper] sincere ... [who] Encourag'd oft, and oft approv'd her lays" (153), to consider imagination to be the *unqualified* poet's understanding or reason, the principle of order, the arranger, organizer, or creator. At the same time Cooper here portrays imagination as a possible mediator between the divine and man. Very likely this last function, and the association of that function with the act of poesis, most appealed to the young Black slave woman become poet.

The poem that immediately follows "On Imagination" in *Poems*, "A Funeral Poem on the Death of C.E. an Infant of Twelve Months," displays unmistakable ties to Wheatley's preceding analysis in "Imagination" of the poet's reason. In her elegy, for example, the departed "wings his instant flight" through "airy roads" "To purer regions of celestial light" (69), much like imagination's swift course through the cosmos to discover "Th' empyreal palace of the thund'ring God" (66). As well, Wheatley's deceased subject, echoing Kames's identification of the most profound expression of the sublime, takes in "the universal whole" wherein "Planets on planets run their destin'd round" (69). Just three pages earlier, "On Imagination" describes a parallel moment in which we as empathetic readers may "in one view . . . grasp the mighty whole" (66). The thought in Cooper's elegy in *Pietas*, then, bespeaks strong connections to Wheatley's own poetic praxis.

Several other links between Wheatley's oeuvre and the *Pietas* volume should be pointed out. In the twenty-eighth poem of the volume, also by Cooper, for example, appear the statements "fan the sacred fire" (86) and "fan the sacred flame" (89). These declarations of poetic afflatus do not occur in Pope, Milton, or Shakespeare, but do closely resemble Wheatley's line in "Hymn to the Morning" about the Muses: Calliope's "fair sisters fan the pleasing fire" (56). Cooper's celebration in this poem of the accession of George III is punctuated throughout with elements of pastoral as he narrates this opportunity for "The Graces and the Virtues [to] join / T'adorn the Royal Train." Here we find "sequester'd bowers," which echo Philomela's (the nightingale's) "thrilling musick," causing "each soft passion of the grove / To charm the royal ear" (87, 88, and 89).

As well, the *Pietas* volume in general makes much of "patriot—virtue[s]" (35, etc.); "silken thought[s]" (16), pointing to Wheatley's "silken fetters" (65); and occasions when "glorious liberty her pinions spread" (23). Throughout the collection the attributive "celestial" recurs with frequency, perhaps encouraging Wheatley's frequent use of this modifier.

William Billings, certainly another American patriot and Wheatley's next close mentor in the evolution of her poetics of the imagination, was America's first native-born composer. His *New-England Psalm-Singer* (1770), a collection of church anthems and songs, enjoyed considerable fame well into the nineteenth century. It has been observed by a mid-nineteenth-century American historian of music that Billings's "Chester," a hymn of intense patriotism, "did more to inspire a spirit of freedom than any one thing that occurred at this critical moment [the American Revolution]" (Gould 44). This hymn's first lyric stanza reads,

> Let Tyrants shake their iron Rod,
> And Slav'ry clank her galling Chains;
> We fear them not, we trust in God,
> New England's God forever reigns! (Billings 321)

With its rhetoric concerning "Tyrants" who enslave, and its clanking, "galling Chains," along with its declaration of strong belief in the Deity, this hymn cannot but have exercised an influence on the young Wheatley.

These two, William Billings and Phillis Wheatley, definitely knew one another. Indeed, Billings collaborated with Wheatley in their shared effort to commemorate the death of Samuel Cooper. Cooper died on December 29, 1783. On January 2, 1784, there appeared an eight-page pamphlet that was prepared for the occasion of Cooper's well-attended funeral. This pamphlet included Wheatley's elegy on Cooper, which we have mentioned; Wheatley's "Elegy . . . [on the] Learned Dr. Samuel Cooper" was followed by a two-page "Anthem" by Billings. Wheatley and Billings probably first met as early as 1769. In October of this year, Billings entered a notice in the *Boston Gazette*:

> John Barry [then Billings's associate] and William Billings Begs [*sic*] Leave to inform the Publick, that they propose to open a Singing School THIS NIGHT, near the Old South Meeting-House, where any Person inclining to learn to Sing may be attended upon at said School with Fidelity and Dispatch. (McKay and Crawford 36)

These Singing Schools were ordinarily attended, "for the duration of three months... mostly [by] young adults and teenagers" (McKay and Crawford 37). Wheatley, about sixteen at the time and given the assurance that "*any Person inclining to learn to sing*" (emphasis added) would be welcome to attend, would have been an ideal candidate for Billings's Singing School. As the "Old South Meeting-House" was the church that the Wheatley family attended and was under the ministry of Wheatley's "monitor," Joseph Sewall (who had died June 27 of the same year), it is most likely that Susannah Wheatley, along with her daughter, Mary, and Phillis herself would have responded positively to this notice. The fact that Billings includes in *The New-England Psalm-Singer* an anthem entitled "Africa," which speaks of "Fears, / Suspicions and complaints," evoking the possibility that Billings herein delivers Wheatley an embedded message regarding her difficulty with Boston's racial prejudice, when combined with the other factors above, multiplies the probability that Wheatley attended Billings's Singing School.

Certainly, the patriotic rhetoric of Billings's anthem, "America," with its sentiments that the American colonies are a land bereft of "Persecution's Iron claws," indeed a country where "Liberty erects her Throne" and "Freedom lift[s] her cheerful Head," would have greatly appealed to Wheatley's identical sentiments, which she expresses in her numerous political, but always patriotic, poems. Given all these indications just enumerated, the probability that Wheatley knew Billings's *New-England Psalm-Singer,* which he used as a tool of instruction in his singing schools, is all but irrefutable. Particularly of interest to this ambitious young poet would have been Billings's brief, prefatory essay, "To all Musical Practitioners," wherein Billings makes several provocative observations regarding the "Rules for Composition" (32).

Billings prescribes, for example, that "*Nature is the best Dictator*" (emphasis in original). "Nature must lay the Foundation" for the air or song (or poem in reference to Phillis Wheatley), so Billings continues. Indeed, "Nature must inspire the Thought. . . . the more Art is display'd, the more Nature is decorated." Billings interestingly exacts no qualifying intervention of judgment or reason, no "manager." When Wheatley remarks in "On Imagination" that "*Fancy* dresses to delight the Muse" (68), she appears to be in agreement with Billings's position that "Art," the artificial creator of the anthem or of a poem, decorates nature herself.

Billings further refines his analytical understanding of the creative process by declaring, "Fancy goes first, and strikes out the Work roughly, and Art comes after, and polishes it over" (32). We have here an inchoate grasp of how the piece of music, or the poem, comes into being, except that in Wheatley, "Art" has become the "imperial queen," imagination. I do not mean to suggest that Billings here draws a clear distinction between fancy and imagination. What he does describe, however, is a line of thought that begins to separate elements of the poetic process into identifiable compartments of responsibility, a responsibility that owes little or nothing to reason or judgment per se, but which somewhat echoes Charron's delineation of memory and fancy as subordinate to imagination.

Billings moves on to state daringly that " . . . if I am not allow'd to transgress the Rules of Composition, I shall certainly spoil the Air, and Cross the Strain, that fancy dictated" (32). To a young but maturing poet, such a liberalizing of the creative process could only have encouraged Wheatley in her personal, interior quest for liberation. Billings expands upon the creative process for poets when he says that he has "felt the disagreeable and slavish Effects" of exterior restraints imposed upon the artist; such restraints have been felt, so Billings holds, by "every composer of Poetry, as well as Musick." Billings reinforces what he sees as a close alliance between poetry and music when he declares that "Poetry and Music are in close connection, and nearly allied, besides they are often assistants to each other and like true friends often hide each others [sic] failings" (32).

One additional pronouncement of Billings that Wheatley would have found compelling is as follows: "I don't think myself confin'd to any Rules for composition laid down by any that went before me" (32). Taking Billings as an authority for composition, whether of music or poetry (and, after all, Billings did compose most of his own lyrics), Wheatley could have, following Billings's lead, found herself liberated all the more, if not in her actual adaptation of form, definitely in her internal choice and handling of poetic subject. When we add to what we have already pulled together about Billings and Wheatley—first that the text of Billings's "America" is actually that of Mather Byles's famous "New-England Hymn" and that Billings eventually became a communicant of Byles's Hollis Street Congregational Church—the relationship between Wheatley and Billings becomes solidified.

Although Wheatley did not regularly attend Byles's Hollis Street Church, that she knew Byles well is virtually donnèe. Both poets deal, in "Eternity" by Byles and in "Thoughts on the Works of Providence" by Wheatley, with subjects of lofty grandeur or sublimity. In these same pieces, Byles and Wheatley both speak of the overwhelmingly sublime image that is, according to Boileau, the pioneer translator of Longinus's *On the Sublime,* the first light of creation as presented in Genesis 1:3: "And God said, Let there be light, and there was light." Byles renders this sublime image in the following manner: "Anon Creation rose in instant Bloom, / And smiling Light dispel'd the horrid Gloom" (*Poems on Several Occasions* 107). Wheatley's persona is even more dazzled by this sublime moment:

> "Let there be light," he said: From his profound
> Old Chaos heard, and trembled at the sound;
> Swift as the word, inspir'd by pow'r divine,
> Behold the light around its maker shine,
> The first fair product of the omnific God,
> And now through all his works diffus'd abroad. (47)

In Wheatley's conception the experience of first light becomes synesthetic; that is, the senses of sight and sound are both evoked, not the sense of sight alone, as in Byles.

Wheatley's construction of a more dramatic and intense image suggests an expansive awareness of the possibilities of the sublime as a manifestation of the enthusiastic powers—not merely as an image of grandeur. Byles uses the word "sublime" seven times in his volume; Wheatley uses the word four times in a body of poems that is far more extensive than that of Byles. But each time Byles uses this word, he always does so as a reference either to the sublime style or to height. He speaks of the language of Milton's *Paradise Lost* as an example of "the true Sublime" (*Poems* 25), and he describes the new home of the deceased Daniel Oliver as "your sublime Abode" (42). Wheatley, however, uses the word "sublime" first to indicate height or loftiness and second to suggest majesty or awe. In "Isaiah lxiii" she characterizes God-like motion as sublime: "Say, heav'nly muse, what king, or mighty God, / That moves sublime from Idumea's road?" (60). Here "sublime" serves not simply as an adverb of place or height but also as an adjective describing the manner of majesty.

Other vocabulary parallels include Byles's "Fancy rove perpetual" (33) and Wheatley's "the roving Fancy flies" (65); the rendering by both poets of the eyes of celestial beings flashing preternatural light (such light imagery ultimately derives in each case most likely from Dante's *Paradiso*); and Byles's "the frozen Floods" (*God Glorious* 15) and Wheatley's "The frozen deeps" (66). Echoes of Byles's vocabulary in Wheatley are too numerous to be accidental. But if they do indicate that Wheatley found Byles's choice of language appealing, they also illustrate that she was an inventive student—one who was generally capable of improving upon her mentor.

Both poets as well build in their works a poetics in which an enthusiastic persona desires ardently to soar, by means of poesy, toward God. In the poem, "To an Ingenious Young Gentleman on His Dedicating a Poem to the Author," which appeared first in the *New England Weekly Journal* in 1727 and later in his 1744 volume, Byles employs a rhetoric of ecstasy in which his persona appears to want to unite with God above. The poem's speaker first dares to "Soar sublime" (52); then Byles states,

> Ravish'd my Ear receives the heav'nly Guest,
> My heart high-leaping, beats my panting Brest:
> Thro' all my Mind incessant Rapture reigns,
> And joys immortal revel in my Veins. (53)

Later in the poem, the thinly veiled persona becomes "Convinc'd, I own Eternity a NOW" (56). Byles concludes this finally abortive attempt at ecstatic unity with God by offering the following, somewhat pompous advice to the "ingenious" young man:

> Thus let your Poesy refine, improve,
> And match the Musick of the Choirs above;
> Still from your Lips let such soft Notes arise,
> And songs of Seraphs sound beneath the Skies,
> Till as your Muse, your Soul expands her Wings,
> And to their bright Abodes, exulting, springs. (56–57)

Byles's prescription of a poetics that matches "the Musick of the Choirs above" suggested to Wheatley an approach to the composition of poetry which offered her temporary relief from a hostile world where she found herself confined as a slave. At an early point in his *Occasions,* Byles has a "Hymn to Christ" which speaks of "ev'ry Sense" (17) and subsequently cites Augustine's triad of memory, reason, and Love: "To Thee my Reason I submit, / My Love, my Mem'ry, Lord" (18). As we have observed, Wheatley too treats memory, understanding, and love as will in "Thoughts on the Works of Providence," though not in the same manner as Byles.

In Wheatley's hands her poetics becomes adapted to her personal predicament and serves her as a source of freedom, a momentary means of escape from harsh reality into the imaginary, happy world of the poem. "On Imagination" demonstrates the power Wheatley attributes to the world of the poem in words that resemble Byles's:

> Soaring through the air to find the bright abode,
> Th' empyreal palace of the thund'ring God,
> We on thy pinions can surpass the wind,
> And leave the rolling universe behind. (66)

Like Byles's, Wheatley's objective is to reach God, but the younger poet strikes a different note in this picture. She maintains that the poem permits the imagination full range; so powerful is the imagination in her poem that it can permit the mind to absent itself from "the rolling universe."

While the older Byles had in his poetry extolled "my wild imagination" (26), the same author, in one of his prose ventures into literary criticism, "Bombastic and Grubstreet Style: A Satire" (appeared first in the *New England Weekly Journal,* April 17, 1727) complained of an "Extravagance of Imagination" (Miller and Johnson 2: 691), predicting Dr. Johnson's exact phrasing later in the century. As well in the same poem in which he had conjured his "wild imagination," he insists in this poem's conclusion that what his imagination has summoned is merely a congeries of "ideal Dreams, / Imaginary Trances! vain Illusions!" (34). Byles, then, like most before him, demanded that imagination be restrained or managed. At another point, the poet soon to become minister remarks the "busy Fancy" (42), once again calling up Pierre Charron. Finally, to Wheatley, however, the power of imagination can even "with new worlds amaze th' unbounded soul" (66). Byles, too, claimed in "To Pictorio" that "at our Word, new Worlds arise" (93). But he does *not,* as Wheatley *does,* move on to construct new worlds. Wheatley's poetics, then, moves into a realm distinct from that of Byles, although he had advanced the aspiration that human poetry could strive toward imitation of angelic song (the music of the spheres).

As Wheatley emphasizes the capacity of poetry to build new, reified worlds, she sees poetry, then, not merely as an imitative activity, but as a potentially mythic, re-creative one. The remainder of "On Imagination" constitutes an attempt to create not one but two new worlds in the face of an unsatisfactory one:

> Though *Winter* frowns to *Fancy's* raptur'd eyes
> The fields may flourish, and gay scenes arise;
> The frozen deeps may break their iron bands,
> And bid their waters murmur o'er the sands. (66)

In the midst of a frowning winter, the power of imagination enables the poet to construct an opposing world of warm spring and, a bit later, another world celebrating the warm sun. But these imaginary worlds can only bring temporary escape; for "northern tempests damp the rising fire; / They chill the tides of *Fancy's* flowing sea" (68). Wheatley's recognition of the power of the imagination to conjure up a new world and of its inevitable failure to sustain this new world anticipates Keats's "Ode to a Nightingale," where the English poet discovers, like she already has, that the wings of poesy provide an escape that is all too brief.

Surely Wheatley's bondage urged upon her this essentially romantic approach to the writing of poetry; certainly her use of "iron bands" as a metaphor for ice can not be construed as accidental. Here as in every other instance cited in this examination of the literary relationship between Byles and our Black poet, Wheatley demonstrates that she surpasses Byles in forcefulness and in imagination. Unlike Byles, who had bade "adieu to the airy Muse," Wheatley pursued the art of poetry as a serious commitment throughout her short adult life.

We come to understand, then, that Wheatley carries with her a far graver burden than Byles, a free white man, would ever be forced to bear. As a woman and a slave, she can not follow Byles into productions of "the airy Muse"; indeed the pleasure she seeks is hardly "airy" but is rather of the highest order—the pleasure, the absolute joy, of liberation. Simply speaking, much more is at stake for this young genius whose regrettable circumstances have thrust her into slavery. Wheatley's intense desire to write comes from within; as she puts it so well, "an intrinsic ardor prompts [me] to write" (15). But this intrinsic ardor alone is not what motivates her to acquire knowledge and to yearn for wisdom and then to articulate in words what life has taught her. She, unlike Byles, is not free.

When we consider how these two express their concerns about imagination, we encounter a radical difference. While Byles at times *appears* to be pro-imagination, he finally characterizes an enthusiastic imagination as delusional. Here Byles actually carries his negative attitude a step or two beyond the many who, as we have observed, required a manager for imagination. To charge imagination with providing the source for trances and "idle Dreams" amounts to one of the most hostile attitudes we have come across, resembling the fanaticism of Jonathan Edwards. Wheatley of course chose a diametrically opposed path, one that elevated imagination to the poet's reason.

British authors and the French Charron were of importance to Wheatley's evolving theoretics of imagination, especially Charron's distinction between fancy and imagination. Her American mentors, Joseph Seccombe (by way of reputation and example), Samuel Cooper, William Billings, and Mather Byles, nevertheless, played far more consequential roles in helping to shape her poetics of imagination. Having investigated those writers who likely or definitely influenced the flowering of Wheatley's imagination theoretics, we are now prepared to turn our attention toward a specific analysis of this poet's construction of that poetics of imagination.

Chapter 3

Wheatley's "Long Poem" and Subsequent Considerations

Critics of the British romantics are fond of focusing attention on the so-called Long Poems of romantic authors—for example, Wordsworth's *Prelude* or Keats's *Endymion*. Such "Long Poems" serve as substantial expressions of what we wish to call "romantic." As three of Wheatley's poems, taken together, do assuredly give shape to her theoretics of the imagination, we may accurately refer to these three works collectively as her "Long Poem." While we have often touched upon the poems that make up Wheatley's "Long Poem," now we examine "On Recollection," "Thoughts on the Works of Providence," and "On Imagination" as a unit. As well, we make occasional excursi into other Wheatley texts as the analysis demands. Wheatley adroitly attests that she is thoroughly engaged with the poetic process—that is, with the act of creating a poem—in "On Recollection," a poem wherein she demonstrates her subtle turn toward interiorization, signaling the first period of her poetic maturity and abandonment of her earlier unsuccessful struggle to find full acceptance with the Boston crowd. This lack of acceptance may well have prompted her revision of "On Recollection" into the excellent, interiorized portrait she gives of her personal struggle during the horrid Middle Passage that brought her to America (on the slaver, the *Phillis,* recall). The first version of this poem dates from late November to early December 1771; the superior revision Wheatley chose to include in her 1773 *Poems*.

In order to accomplish the five-stress iambic line of heroic verse, Wheatley opts to open "Recollection" with the older form of memory's name, "Mneme," rather than choosing the four-syllable, less ancient "Mnemosyne." Hence Wheatley suggests her sophistication as a classicist. This faculty, of course gendered female, is, according to Wheatley, one of power. Recognizing Mneme as an "immortal pow'r," Wheatley calls up "Thy pow'r" (l. 7), "thy pow'r" (l. 38) again, and "her pow'r," in order finally to assert her own power in application of this faculty; it is, after all, the power of her own memory that summons "from night" "the long-forgotten" (l. 7). Upon first encounter, this powerful faculty "sweetly plays before the *fancy's* sight" (l. 8). To Wheatley this play becomes most manifest as "nocturnal visions" that Mneme "pours" into the mind, wherein an "ample treasure" of separate memories registers as "secret stores." Mneme's "stores" arrange themselves as a "pomp of images display'd" that give "to the high-raptur'd poet" assistance in the construction of her poems.

Of great significance is that Wheatley insists that this treasure trove of images occupies "the unbounded regions of the mind." This insistence establishes that this poet's memory, which knows no bounds, is free to explore without restraint—that is, bereft of the chains of slavery. Such a perspective here points directly to Wheatley's liberation poetics. Interestingly, Charron had earlier held that "Memory acts not at all but is purely Passive" (Charron, Stanhope ed. 19), this passage possibly serving as a source for Coleridge's description of fancy/memory in chapter 13 of *Biographia Literaria* (305). To the renaissance skeptic, imagination "collects together the Ideas and Figures of Things"; at this early point in Wheatley's evolving poetics, her enthusiasm for memory's "immortal pow'r" leads her to ascribe to Mneme what she would soon hold to be the responsibility of fancy. Later she would invest memory with less "pow'r."

In "Recollection," nevertheless, the poet names memory "The heaven'ly *phantom* [who] paints the actions done / By ev'ry tribe beneath the rolling sun" (ll. 17–18). Wheatley is going to present, then, a sweeping panorama that condemns vice and praises virtue. "Virtue" brings to her mind sounds "Sweeter than music to the ravish'd ear," which recall to her the "entertaining strains" of Virgil's Latin eclogues, "Resounding through the groves, and hills, and plains" (ll. 22–24). From this representation of idyllic pastoral, the poet shifts quickly, but *apparently* innocuously, to the realm of vice in which memory unveils "each horrid crime" attended by "Days, years misspent" conjuring "a hell of woe!" This woeful hell summons "the worst tortures that our souls can know" (ll. 27–30).

After a casual reading, one is inclined to think, because the poet declares that her memory causes these horrid crimes to return, hence provoking her "to be asham'd, and mourn," that the crimes are probably her own. Closer inspection, however, "paints" quite a different picture. Indeed what would an asthmatic, benign teenager closely supervised by her white owners know of "the worst tortures"? Recall that Phillis, gallingly and unimaginatively named for the slaver that brought her, was seven or eight years old when she was sold on the block, July 11, 1761, with nothing but a piece of dirty carpet to conceal her nakedness. So she was certainly old enough to have recorded implacably on her memory the horrors of the terrible Middle Passage. Acknowledging that the mores governing the behavior of young African girls would have universally demanded these female children exercise modesty, one can readily grasp why the young girl's piece of dirty carpet would have forced shame upon her.

As for her mourning, this innocent victim of slavery no doubt possessed a plethora of occasions for her grief, such as the loss of her parents, siblings, and other family members, not to mention the loss or possible deaths of those Africans who befriended her on the wretched journey from Africa to Boston. Viewed from this perspective, Wheatley's ostensibly sweeping prospect actually bespeaks an intensely personal experience, virtually unmatchable by any whites in her adoptive Boston. Using the pastoral world of Vergil's eclogues, which always hold the possibility of subversion, Wheatley, while looking harmless, has accomplished the construction of a powerful indictment of slavery. The poet's experience of the follies (which in Joshua 7:15 and Judges 20:6 of the KJV referred to evil[s], sin[s], or crime[s]) of "eighteen years" have passed, to the white folks, "Unnotic'd." But, so she continues, now we "behold them writ in brass!" In Shakespeare's *Henry VIII,* the English bard has the lines, as we have noted, "Men's evil manners live in brass, their virtues / We write in water" (4.2.45–46). (The writing in water brings to mind Keats's requested epitaph, "Here lies one whose life was writ in water.") We may, then, readily conclude that this most clever and well-read poet has, in "On Recollection," written anything but an innocuous tract, for as Wheatley so pointedly admonishes, "The wretch [a white enslaver], who dar'd the vengeance of the skies, / At last awakes in horror and surprise" (ll. 43–44).

"Thoughts on the Works of Providence," the second member of her "Long Poem," which advances Wheatley's quest for a poetics of imagination a few steps further, arguably falls into the realm of the *meditatio* or meditation, emphasizing that, from the days of ancient classicism, the major faculties of the mind have consisted of memory, understanding, and will. The ancients, as we have learned, traditionally divided memory into a subtrinity: the senses, the appetites, and the imagination. Hence, once again the poet is concerned to treat "unbounded space" (l. 22), "misspent time" resulting in a need to mourn folly or evil/sin (ll. 67–68), and a condition of creativity in which the poet soars in a state of "rapture" (l. 45). Opening the poem with a ten-line invocation, her first of two ten-line invocations, hence suggesting the significance of this exercise of the mind, Wheatley establishes that the "monarch of the earth and skies" will serve as her locus or necessary location on which to focus her attention (à la *Ars memorativa*); this process of establishing a locus is, according to classical rhetoric (whence the meditative process originates), the first step governing the *meditatio*. This focus upon the sun (with a possible pun on Son, though Wheatley here makes no mention of Jesus or Christ) enables Wheatley to treat two attendant concerns: the vastness of space and the importance of wisdom (recall Charron's *De la sagesse* or *On Wisdom*).

Wheatley's concentration on wisdom in "Thoughts" is underscored by the likelihood that she may have, in her pursuit or study of Joseph Seccombe, come across another of Seccombe's published sermons, *A Specimen of the Harmony of Wisdom and Felicity* (1743). In this homily, which, as we have observed of Seccombe before, resembles a treatise more than a sermon, Seccombe states in his preface that "By Wisdom Man knows himself and is humble, acquaints himself with Men and pays Deference to every one according to Desert." Reflecting gentlemanly desire to achieve wisdom and happiness in a secular world, Seccombe's disposition would have served the maturing poet most constructively as a guide toward the adoption of a well-functioning, even diplomatic demeanor.

Surely Wheatley's poetic persona in "Thoughts" bespeaks, at least on the surface, a preoccupation with appearing to be humble and diplomatic as the poet pursues the burden of providing her readers, white and Black, instruction in the quest for a wise disposition. As in the earlier "On Recollection," Wheatley again takes up consideration of the force of "nocturnal visions." In "Thoughts," however, the poet displays progress in her thinking. "As reason's pow'rs by day our God disclose," writes the poet, "So we may trace him in the night's repose." Notice that Wheatley has not yet concluded that imagination is the poet's reason, as she would do in the later "On Imagination."

Her movement into the seemingly harmless world of sleep/dream, however, suggests an advance in her theoretics, for in a state of sleep/dream, daily, quotidian "action ceases" but "ideas range / Licentious and unbounded o'er the plains." In other words, the "unbounded space" of the exterior universe, which provokes an awestruck response to the God of nature, becomes a kind of mirror for her focus on redirecting her attention to that interiorization which points toward the limitless realm of the human mind, particularly this poet's mind. While the exterior world of Boston, for example, would confine her in the shackles of slavery, Wheatley claims ownership of her own interior, limitless mind. In this interior world, which also knows no bounds, we discover that "Fancy's queen in giddy triumph reigns" (ll. 83–88). Here Wheatley predicts the "imperial queen" of "On Imagination," just as she sets up a relationship between the mental functions of fancy and imagination, wherein fancy becomes subordinate to the superior, imperial imagination.

Hence, in "Thoughts," Wheatley has turned an ostensible search for wisdom into an exercise in self-discovery. The ultimate objective of the meditative process is, indeed, to bring about precisely such an interior discovery of self. "Thoughts," then, has provided Wheatley the opportunity to explore the faculties of her own mind as she engages the "powers" of memory, wherein she finds her focus on the exterior God of nature; the understanding, which enables her to refocus her attention on individual "power" to discover her own limitless mind; and finally her will which becomes manifest in her creation of "Thoughts" (memory, understanding, and will identify the tripartite structure of the *meditatio*). Herein she has come to realize that the engagement of the meditative process constitutes her central means of internal empowerment.

"On Imagination," the last portion of her "Long Poem," thoroughly enacts Wheatley's discovery of her individual empowerment over her own poetic creations. As pertains to her entire, extant poetry, "On Imagination" surely exemplifies her pièce de résistance. This complicated poem was certainly touted in the years following her premature death on December 5, 1784, as her best work. Here her debt to Charron and others comes to an abrupt end. Despite Charron's division of the mind into understanding, memory, and imagination, in significant contradistinction to the ancients, despite his hedging separations of fancy and imagination wherein fancy serves imagination, and despite British and American eighteenth-century aesthetic theorists who preceded, and probably (several definitely) were examined by, Wheatley regarding their use of imagination, this excellent and original poet follows a course plotted by her own, individual needs and aspirations.

In the first three stanzas of "On Imagination," Wheatley establishes a tension between imagination, whom she names the "imperial queen" in the first line, and the "roving Fancy." Whereas imagination produces multiple "works" (poems) and bright forms that stand "in beauteous order," all demonstrating the overriding power of this faculty, the fancy flits here and there, as if on a mission to affix upon "some lov'd object" to bring into focus the mind's eye of the poet. It would appear that it is the province of the fancy to bind all the senses, thereby captivating the mind by means of "silken fetters."

While Wheatley appropriated the phrase "silken fetters" from Mark Akenside's 1744 *Pleasures of the Imagination,* wherein he has the line, "The silken fetters of delicious ease" (book 2, l. 562), this phrase in Wheatley's hands bears at least double meaning. To a slave, fetters are, perhaps, just chains; yet *these* chains are indeed silken, and more importantly they are imposed by choice of the poet on the operation of her own mind in the act of creation. Thereby they become manifestations of her own agency and, if you will, of her own intellectual property. So the bow toward white enslavement registers on a minimal level, if at all. Most cleverly Wheatley has accomplished in her application of this phrase a metaphor of liberating empowerment, not one of debilitating restriction.

The next line, "*Imagination!* who can sing thy force?" makes a radical break away from the notion of a "roving *Fancy.*" This powerful faculty can soar through the air, emphasizing the cosmic possibilities for this faculty, and even discover "the bright abode . . . of the thundering God." These ventures into cosmic flight conjure up Longinus, Shakespeare, Akenside, and the young Freneau (his "Power of Fancy," which remains firmly in the realm of associative psychology). Perhaps this God of thunder is the Old Testament Jehovah; perhaps he is Jupiter, god of thunderbolts. The reference, probably deliberately, remains ambiguous. Wheatley is next careful to propose that "We," she and her readers, can, on wings of poesy, "surpass the wind / And leave the rolling universe behind." From this immense expanse, we can each grasp in a single view "the mighty whole."

Then the poet collapses this cosmic perspective, as we have seen in "Thoughts," in order to capture a completely interior moment of discovery. As she puts it so well, "Or with new worlds amaze th' unbounded soul" (ll. 13–21). What is particularly stunning here is that next Wheatley proceeds to construct a completely secular heterocosm, an alternative world. From a dynamic description of the feeling of the sublime, she rapidly descends into the interior realm of her own mind; this great rapidity of movement from the cosmic to the mind's interior predicts Kant's description in his "Analytic of the Sublime" of a pattern of vibrations between the object or expanse contemplated and the mind in the act of contemplation. The poet has here attempted, by use of her imagination, to bridge the gap between a vision of the divine, the "imperial palace," and the secular world of warm pastoral.

Wheatley, in seizing this moment of interiorization as an opportunity to build a new world, has taken the poet's license to exceed vibratory movement and to linger for a time in a delightful realm of happy, earthlike images, all of which are assuredly absent of any hint of slavery. As she has it, "Though *Winter* frowns to Fancy's raptur'd eye," she will use her poet's mind, her "mental optics," to shape a world of flourishing fields and "gay scenes," sounding much like Vergil's pastoral or perhaps even a nostalgic recollection of her native Gambia. In "On Recollection," fancy is a faculty (subfaculty) of sight that focuses on a memory which "plays" before and thereby assists "the high-raptur'd poet" in fashioning her poem. Here, however, the fancy is itself the agent that intensifies the poet's vision of the new world; this functioning as an intensifier is consistent with fancy as a captivator who binds "all the senses" in stanza 3. As in "Recollection," then, we view the poet as having achieved an ecstatic state of creativity. But it is the imperial queen who, with the fancy's aid, supervises the "wond'rous acts" of the poet—that is, her poems, and finally produces a "beauteous order."

The frowning winter evocative of forbidding cold conjures a perhaps inevitable parallel to the Boston white folks, especially those who hold slaves, including John and Susanna Wheatley; the necessity to search for and find a warm realm bereft of slavery, therefore, becomes acute. In Wheatley's secular heterocosm, "The frozen deeps may break their iron bands, / And bid their waters murmur o'er the sands." In this alternate world, cold, inhospitable winter warms to a temperate summer wherein fields may bear new life; release from the white folks' cold bondage produces a fecund fertility wholly free of stultifying, disabling shackles. Just so Wheatley has now pointedly applied her creative mind to the task of achieving liberation—first and foremost, of course, for herself, but excluding no one.

Although forbidding "*Winter*" may look with scorn on the ecstatic, wondrous production of the poet, Wheatley's heterocosm exhibits warm waters that "murmur o'er the sands," perhaps echoing the strand along Wheatley's native Gambia. Significantly, the innocuous-sounding "Fair *Flora*" vaunts "her fragrant reign" and decks the plain with "her flow'ry riches," evoking the "Licentious and unbounded" ideas ranged "o'er the plains" in "Thoughts," though the earlier abstract ideas here enact concrete expression. In this poet's alternative world, "*Sylvanus,*" another harmless-looking figure from ancient classicism, joins Flora as he crowns the forest trees with leaves.

When we discover, however, that, according to William King's immensely popular *An Historical Account of the Heathen Gods and Heroes,* which appeared in 1710 and was readily available to Wheatley (Robert Middlekauff, for example, records that by 1752 King's *Heathen Gods* had become a standard text in the Boston Latin grammar school [Middlekauff 85–86]), "Flora was a Courtezan, who got a great sum of Money by her immodest Practices" but willed her fortune to the people of Rome "upon condition that the Games called Floralia might be celebrated annually on her Birth-day" (193). Sylvanus, who was, again according to King, "always in the company of Pan," was god of "the Woods and Shepherds, and the Boundaries of Land" (186). His office actually was to rule over wild, uncultivated lands. So Flora as a prostitute connotes profligacy or, as in "Thoughts," licentiousness, and Sylvanus as the god in charge of that realm outside urban confines—that is, the wild, unregulated forests and uncultivated fields beyond the limits of civilization—conjures a world of disorder, certainly not given, nevertheless, to the sadly calculated practice of slavery. What may appear on the surface to be harmless proves to be the precise opposite. And Sylvanus's association with Pan, well known for his sexual exploits, also serves as a link to Flora's sexual abandon.

We should add, nevertheless, that, on the one hand, Flora did represent the beauty of flowers and therefore of pastoral warmth and, on the other, that Sylvanus was clearly associated with wisdom, sometimes called the wise old man of the forest, and through Pan was a supporter of music. Wheatley has, then, depicted in the first of her two heterocosms a strikingly complex vision, one of course with no hint of slavery. Her poetics of liberation is surely alive and quite well in this ostensibly trouble-free arena, which promises both beauty and pleasure and an unlimited space wherein the poet can pursue the unbounded limits of her individual imagination—all constituting a kind of poetic paradise.

In the next stanza, the poet moves, one believes with reluctance, from gems of dew and sparkling nectar on blooming roses to celebration of the powerful imagination as unchallenged "leader of the mental train." So powerful, recall the power of memory, has imagination now become to Wheatley that imagination, without qualification (no manager) casts reifications of her abstract thoughts into "full perfection." Indeed in this perfect world, even the "subject-passions bow," for "Of subject-passions sov'reign ruler Thou." This somewhat puzzling assertion becomes clear when we discover that, in Pope's "Epistel to Bathurst" (1733), passion connotes, in the eighteenth century, "the Motives of Avaricious men" (176); surely to this female slave, the most compelling manifestation of avarice was embodied in the institution of slavery, as is the case in Pope's "Epistle." In Wheatley's perfect world, then, even despised slavery disappears; for as she most affectively puts it, at the command of her imagination, "joy rushes on the heart."

The intensity of Wheatley's moral vision in these lines must not go unremarked. Indeed as she calls her *Poems . . . Moral,* here as in the earlier "On Recollection," Wheatley summarily condemns the practice of slavery. In *Imagination under Pressure, 1789–1832: Aesthetics, Politics, and Utility,* John Whale emphatically asserts of his revisionist evaluation of British romanticism that the imagination "inhabits a particular moral and ethical space" (195). Certainly we can now declare that Wheatley's sensibility resides firmly within just such a "moral and ethical space." If Wheatley's British and Continental audiences could grasp her condemnation of the hated institution, their enthusiasm for reading her often reprinted texts far exceeded mere curiosity; her texts may well have helped to promote the later Romantics' great moral preoccupation, particularly regarding freedom for all human beings.

To return to "On Imagination," not yet fully satisfied that she has sufficiently exercised the power of her imagination, the poet proceeds next to construct still another heterocosm, this second depiction probably kindled by the preceding "joy" which darts through her "glowing veins." Now fancy as agent of mental involvement sweeps "th' expanse on high" and fastens on Aurora, always in Wheatley evocative of her memory of her beloved mother. (If the reader finds my "always" extreme, know that I should be pleased to be proven wrong.) This particular citation of Aurora (Wheatley calls up the dawn on numerous occasions, even writing "An Hymn to the Morning") is accompanied by Tithonus, perhaps the dawn's most beloved paramour. As Aurora leaves "Tithon's bed," her "cheeks all glowing with celestial dies," her light produces "a pure stream." These images of her mother's dawn occupy the space of a triplet, the only one in the poem, thereby bringing special importance to its content. Why? When we discover that the union of Tithonus and Aurora produced Memnon, a prince of Ethiopia, and that Wheatley was fond of calling herself "an Ethiop," this heterocosm assumes personal significance. If Aurora represents her mother, then Wheatley figuratively becomes Memnon's sister, hence her proudly naming herself an Ethiop. The upshot of such a claim, even if subversively made, strongly suggests the great importance Wheatley attaches to this experiment in poetics.

This second heterocosm allows the poet next to behold the "monarch of the day," recalling the "monarch of th' ethereal train" (43) in "Thoughts," who here tips "all the mountains … with radiant gold." The ecstasy of this second reified, mythical world is short-lived, however, as the poet acknowledges, now with unmistakable reluctance, that she cannot indefinitely sustain her mythical worlds. But note that Wheatley carefully tells us in this poem's concluding lines that the "*Fancy*" has dressed these worlds "to delight the *Muse*." Most regretfully now, "Winter austere forbids me to aspire." The white folks who earlier frowned on her enraptured vision now demand that her adventure "Cease." Note, nevertheless, that it is finally only by her own edict that she brings the poem to a close: "Cease, then, my song, cease the unequal lay."

This somewhat troubling last line does not leave the reader with a perfectly clear motive for her conclusion. Indeed, what is "unequal" about her song? Does this comment, "unequal lay," serve as a subversive complaint regarding her social status? Is her poem unequal to the task of long sustaining a mythical world? Even the Keats of "Ode to a Nightingale" finally has to abandon his beloved bird's song. In any event, Wheatley has in "On Imagination" accomplished the composition of a powerful explication regarding the operation of her own imagination. Her identification of imagination as "leader of the mental train" enacts a revolutionary moment in the evolution of literary aesthetics. While the Early Americans, Samuel Cooper and William Billings, levy enthusiastic observations about imagination, it is time that we all give Phillis Wheatley the credit due her for being the first to recognize imagination as occupying the highest rank among a poet's faculties, hence serving as the poet's reason.

Unquestionably this revolutionary elevation of imagination points directly to the several romanticisms of the Continent and of Great Britain. While Wheatley's "Long Poem" displays the romantic and, for her time, revolutionary indications enumerated above, when we combine the contributions of the "Long Poem" with additional examples, also redolent of romanticism, from her entire oeuvre, we discover still more fascinating and substantial prefigurations of the British and Continental romanticisms. These prefigurations include, but are not limited to, Wheatley's intense and pronounced opposition to slavery; her pursuit in her poetry of her own idea of God; her use of nature as an inspirer of self-revelation; her capacity to harness the power of her own imagination to provide her access to new truths and knowledge, leading to a perception that such new knowledge may empower her to overcome her confinement, this process resulting in the creation of a literature of power predicting De Quincey; her emphasis on the internal struggle of an individual's search for meaning in an unsatisfactory, hostile world; her drawing out of how the unconscious functions as an inspiration for creativity; her use of what Peter Otto has aptly phrased "aesthetic order to disguise political disorder" (381) as demonstrated by her subversive rebellion against slavery and gender bias; and her pioneering of the woman's role in advancing the development of British and Continental romanticisms.

I should like my readers to know that I am not herein attempting to define "romanticism." I am, moreover, well aware of how contentious the critical furor over this elusive subject has become. Not at all wishing to enter this unstable arena, what I am trying to describe is just how often Wheatley's "Long Poem," particularly, accords with what *others* have called "romantic" about the several romanticisms. I have in mind such authorities as Meyer H. Abrams, Walter Jackson Bate, Peter Otto, Jack Stillinger, Francis Gallaway, William Harmon and C. Hugh Holman, Iain McCalman, John Whale, Marshall Brown, and Antony Flew, all of whom I cite within this monograph.

Wheatley's concern for human rights, especially as related to slavery, is by now surely well known and requires only a brief rehearsal. In "To Maecenas," the poem that opens her 1773 *Poems,* Wheatley expresses a thinly veiled concern for her own enslavement in the phrase "The happier Terence" (11). Indeed Terence, the ancient Roman playwright of sophisticated comedies of manner who early on in his career was a slave and, according to Wheatley's own footnote, "an African by birth," is happier than the author because the success of his pen has brought about his freedom, although Wheatley is herself still a slave and therefore "less happy." The earlier "On Recollection," as we have recognized, presents a much more heavily veiled assessment of the despised institution. Wheatley's clever masking of her severe condemnation of slavery has already been treated, and many have remarked on Wheatley's protest in "To the . . . Earl of Dartmouth." Here in a poem devoted to "Fair Freedom," the poet affectingly places a memory of her unhappy abduction from her father's arms, which has resulted in her personal knowledge of the "tyrannic sway" which has denied her "Fair Freedom."

Following the award of her freedom shortly before October 18, 1773, motivated by, according to her own testimony, "the desire of my friends in England" (Wheatley strongly suggests that her master, John Wheatley, required prompting from abroad, to address her "less happy" condition), Wheatley attacked the Colonial American contradictory stance that condoned slavery but lamented the alleged enslavement of white colonials by Great Britain. In this same missive, addressed to the Mohegan minister and Dartmouth graduate Samson Occom, but printed in almost a dozen Colonial American newspapers, Wheatley intones an eloquent and candid declaration of freedom when she writes: " . . . in every human Breast, God has implanted a Principle, which we call Love of Freedom; it is impatient of Oppression and it pants for Deliverance." She then adds " . . . by Leave of our Modern Egyptians I will assert, that the same Principle lives in us" (177).

Note that in this letter of February 11, 1774, dated within four months of her manumission letter, Wheatley has dropped her subversive posture altogether. As well, she employs the apt metaphor of the biblical Israelites and their predicament as they exited from Egyptian enslavement. In this, her most candid and public condemnation of slavery, she forcefully uses the plural, first-person pronouns "we" and "us," not hesitating to align herself with her Black brothers and sisters. Nonetheless, even today some people claim that Wheatley ignored the plight of her race.

Unfortunately, such later abolitionists as Thomas Clarkson and Granville Sharp in England, and William Lloyd Garrison and Frederick Douglass in America appear to have been unaware of Wheatley's most significant prose tract. The slavery issue, nevertheless, is not the only human rights concern Wheatley shoulders in her work. That she was committed to equality of the sexes is signaled by the demonstrated fact that she promotes again and again female principals as goddesses and as gendered intellectual aesthetic concepts; in another venue I have provided a detailed examination of Wheatley's repeated glorification of goddess figures (see *The American Aeneas,* ch. 6), and we have observed that our poet has gendered fancy, imagination, "Love," "Reason," and recollection all as female principals. We will take up the gender issue again shortly.

Another preoccupation that Wheatley's work manifests which predicts the later romantics is her pursuit of religious freedom. This preoccupation becomes most apparent in her syncretization of elements of classicism, solar worship, animism, Islam, and Judeo-Christianity. Each of these approaches to religious consciousness I have elaborated in *Phillis Wheatley's Poetics of Liberation* (see ch. 5). The salient point to be made here is that such a broadly based religious consciousness argues that this excellent poet was *not* limited by any particular religious dogma. Contrary to misinformed perspectives, Wheatley was simply not a "safe" subscriber to Christianity alone. As is the case with other minds of genius, this artist's idea of God was always sincere but not a testimony to any single, formal religion. In other words, she was not, in the strict sense, a Congregationalist.

Perhaps as we may expect from one not limited by dogma (the purpose of dogma is ever to stop thinking, but Wheatley appeared not to be pleased by the application of chains upon her mind), Wheatley's frame of mind toward nature at times seems to approach a Wordsworthian pantheism (see Harmon and Holmes 374–75; but see Fry's tempered treatment in *Wordsworth,* 26, 143–44). Certainly we have observed in "Thoughts on the Works of Providence" the operation of a keen capacity to find in Nature a profound occasion to adopt a worshipful attitude. I submit we must be quick to say, moreover, that, since we have no mention of Christianity or Christ per se in this piece, this attitude bespeaks something resembling a secular perspective, while at the same time Wheatley's perspective affects an awed response. In this awed response, we may discover a species of natural sublime pointing directly to the Kant of "Analytic of the Sublime" and the later romantics.

In "Thoughts," for example, Wheatley's projection of the Deity's creative power in nature moves her to contemplate the creative power of her own mind. After she investigates the power of her own mind within sleep, she asks, "What secret hand returns the mental train / And gives improv'd thine active pow'rs again?" (48). The God of nature aligns itself with "the mental train" of our poet in order to activate an improved state for her own mental train—that is, to create within the poet the power of poetic productivity (for origins of Wheatley's use of "train," see Shields, *Phillis Wheatley's Poetics of Liberation* 88, 151–52, and 155–56).

Coleridge would, in his 1825 *Aids to Reflection*, assert that the productive power of imagination enables minds of genius among literary artists to project a form (as in their works of art) of "the artist's own being," according to Peter Otto's phrasing in his excellent discussion of Coleridge's *Aids*. The artist herein taps into a "transcendent creative power which is the absolute ground of both nature and the self." "At the same time," the artist's creative productions become "a sign of the creative power of Nature or God" (Otto 383). Uncannily, Wheatley has anticipated Coleridge by over fifty years.

As has been implicitly stated above, what Wheatley will shortly identify as her imagination has in "Thoughts" empowered her to gain access to new knowledge. In other words, her imagination has led her to recognize in her own mind a means toward self-revelation. Indeed, Wheatley's turn inward has granted her the knowledge, actually the power, to overcome a painful world "Oppress'd with woes" (152).

In this sense, Wheatley accomplishes the projection of a truth beyond ordinary reality, for she has discovered that the mind of human beings can and often must rise above petty avarice that would bring only injury to the innocent. As we have observed earlier, the works of Providence are "array'd with mercy" and are in their natural condition bereft of slavery. Wheatley's poetic undertaking would appear to illustrate, then, an example of De Quincey's literature of power, in the sense that Wheatley has in this poem succeeded in conveying what De Quincey terms one of "the higher functions of literature," this clearly reaching beyond the delivery of mere information. In "Thoughts," Wheatley moves her readers to recognize that, as De Quincey declares, "there is a rarer thing than truth—namely, *power*, or deep sympathy with truth" (Abrams and Stillinger 548).

While, as we have seen, Wheatley relishes the prospect of pursuing universal truths, she was also much concerned to explore the possibility of her own individual feeling. Her ability to relate her individual, personal feeling we may easily find in another instance of her great appreciation for nature. Rather than the sweeping expanses in "Thoughts" of the celebration of sublime natural wonders, now we encounter another manifestation of Wheatley's intense turn inward. In "An Hymn to the Morning," the poet tells of the "Harmonious lays" of nature's birds that signal the approach of the dawn. The break of day becomes poignantly apparent, not merely in the sounds of the birds' singing, but in the interplay of the birds' eyes with the coming light. As she puts it marvelously, "Dart the bright eye, and shake the painted plume" (56). We know the birds' eyes "dart" because we see the reflection of the coming light picked up by the observers' eyes as the birds' eyes move about. This kind of close observation bespeaks a deep appreciation of natural phenomena, while also conjuring up Aristotle's tracing of the origin of phantasia to that which empowers the eye to perceive light.

As well, the darting eyes and painted plumes (an African memory?) convey a close capacity to recognize in Wheatley's imagery an expression of individual response and sentiment. We need not belabor the fact that this poet's close observations display what Walter Jackson Bate in *From Classic to Romantic: Premises of Taste in Eighteenth-Century England* has called "a tendency to emphasize the fundamental importance of individual feeling or sentiment" (128). Indeed, Wheatley's numerous elegies present a plethora of sentiments for both the loss and celebration of the departed. Still another example (many more could be summoned) of Wheatley's intensely emotional response becomes evident in this poet's repeated reverence for her mother; I refer to her use of imagery related to the dawn of her beloved mother as is obvious in the morning "Hymn."

Wheatley's emphasis on her individual struggle to discover to herself knowledge and meaning we may observe in her analysis of the workings of her own subconscious. Like the romantics who followed her, Wheatley sought to explain to herself, if not to her readers, what Bate terms the "romantic conception of the imagination as . . . comprising the use, with unusual intensity and instinctive facility, of the total unconscious mind" (116). As we have mentioned, Wheatley explores analytically how the mind functions during sleep in "Thoughts on the Works of Providence." In the somewhat earlier "On Recollection," Wheatley first presents an analysis of how the subconscious empowers the poet, this particular poet, to store secret treasures for later use by the creative consciousness in the construction of a poem.

As she puts it, "Mneme [memory] in our nocturnal visions [dreams] pours / The ample treasure of her secret stores" (62). This "treasure" provides her a "pomp of images display'd" which "To the high-raptur'd poet gives her aid."

These images become exploited by the poet as she builds her poem. But note that, as before, these images reside in "the unbounded regions of the mind" where they diffuse "light celestial and refin'd." So to this poet, Mneme or memory, Mother of the Muses, dwells in a limitless realm, one that encourages and even works in concert with the mind of the poet to create the poem. We should recall that, by the time of "On Imagination," memory has surrendered much of her "immortal power" (62) to the supreme, imperial queen, imagination. Observe, nevertheless, that within the realm of memory, stored images come forth, emanating a heavenly, purified radiance. Perhaps this purification process was, for Wheatley, necessary, for what she subsequently "paints" (63) are the evils of slavery. My point is to suggest that only a process of purification of those terrible memories will allow Wheatley now to record them.

Such recollection of the terrible institution doubtless directed Wheatley's attention, in accord with her turn inward characterizing the first period of her poetic maturity, toward Peter Otto's identification of the romantics' use of "aesthetic order to disguise political disorder." Wordsworth's poetry enacts a worthy illustration of this process, but so do many of Wheatley's postjuvenile poems. "On Imagination," to be sure, glorifies such a process. Indeed, while the "various works" of the "imperial queen" become "deck'd with pomp by thee!" all "Thy wond'rous acts in beauteous order stand." These "wond'rous acts," her poems, are wondrous simply because the fact that one enslaved can produce poems at all is, of course, a miracle. Most significantly these poems she has "made" stand in a "beauteous order" because they sustain no slavery. The chaos brought about by mankind's avarice has, as we have seen, been cast out by this feeling, compassionate poet.

That Wheatley shapes her poems in a calculated, orderly manner is signaled by the regularity of the heroic couplet. The fact that each of the three poems constituting her "Long Poem" assumes the loose form of the lyric, Horatian ode, however, mitigates the strict rhythm of their closed couplets. So we observe a somewhat startling contradiction in this poet's adaptation of form. The contradiction may be easily enough explained first because the regularity of rhythm enabled, or helped to enable, the poet to affect a clear order in the midst of potential chaos. In addition, this "look" of order assisted Wheatley in her subversive undertaking to give her overwhelmingly white readers the appearance of innocuousness; had she "looked" bolder—that is, had she adopted the looser stanzas of a Collins, for example—her rebellious theoretics may have been more readily detectable.

Another manifestation of Wheatley's "look" of harmlessness may be viewed in her advancement of the feminine. Given the fact that women poets as elegists exercised, in her native Africa, complete control over the elegiac form (see ch. 4 in Shields, *Phillis Wheatley's Poetics of Liberation*), Wheatley may well have been encouraged to challenge the status of women, both in Boston and in England. Her consistent glorification of female goddesses, from Aurora (redolent of her beloved mother) to Phoebe, and Imagination to Recollection, declare a powerful appreciation for the woman's part.

Another example of Wheatley's independence of mind resulting in a raising up of the artistic and even economic capacities of women becomes obvious from the fact that our poet fully intends to make a gainful vocation of her poetic talents. For example, in the month of her manumission letter, she urges her friend and soul mate (à la William Robinson), Obour Tanner, to use her influence to acquire subscriptions for her 1773 volume, "as it is for my benefit" (172). Indeed in her manumission letter of October 18, 1773, addressed to David Wooster, later to become an American general in the Revolution, Wheatley discusses the disposition of the 1773 volume in some detail. Noting that she expected the arrival of some three hundred more of her books within "8 or 10 days," now she seizes the opportunity to solicit from Wooster not only his endorsement of her *Poems,* but his active participation in ferreting out subscriptions for her book: "I am now on my own footing and whatever I get by this is entirely mine & it is the chief I have to depend on." She also allows Wooster to know that she is "to have half the Sale of the Books" (170).

At a time when most authors still continued to depend on literary patrons (despite Samuel Johnson's declaration of financial independence), Wheatley, now a freed woman, but a woman nonetheless, announces that her manumission has thrust her onto the stage of economic necessity. What a courageous woman! Had the American Revolution not come about, she may well have succeeded in her bid for financial independence. That she was solicitous of her economic welfare, essentially becoming a feminine rebel by serving as her own Maecenas; that she was a promulgator of powerful female principles; and particularly that she promoted a new way of employing the poet's reason, or the imagination, strongly argue for recognizing this woman poet as a pioneer of women's rights, at least in the literary arena, and therefore a worthy predictor of Mary Wollstonecraft, who was later involved in publishing Gilbert Imlay's *Topographical Description of the North American Continent.*

Wheatley advances the woman's part in yet another substantial way. In 1807 William Duff, whom we have met before, published *Letters on the Intellectual and Moral Character of Women,* in which he claimed not ever to have encountered "any instances of a 'powerful imagination'" among women writers (McCalman 553). Even if he knew of Wheatley's *Poems,* which had enjoyed at least six London printings by 1807, he obviously did not take her seriously. It is, nonetheless, certain that Wheatley's analysis and promotion of imagination as the supreme faculty of the poet's mind puts Duff's assertion to the lie. As well, and perhaps even more significantly, Wheatley's poetics of imagination, along with her glorification of woman, explodes the command held by the patriarchal authority regarding understanding of the imagination, heretofore granted exclusively to male authors of the romantic period.

We could pepper our investigation of Wheatley's romantic connections with still other examples. Her concern with ekphrasis, a popular romantic preoccupation, in "Niobe in Distress for Her Children Slain by Apollo, from Ovid's *Metamorphoses,* Book VI and from a View of the Painting of Mr. Richard Wilson" (Wheatley actually saw this painting while visiting the Earl of Dartmouth during her London visit) and in "To S.M. a Young African Painter, on Seeing His Works," is of course evident in these poems' titles. Her use of her poems as a kind of therapy (as in Wordsworth's using sections of *The Prelude* as "an antidote to the dislocations and artifice of modernity" [McCalman 553]) is most evident in her search for order in a world that permits slavery. That she sometimes breaks the rules, probably encouraged by William Billings, assuredly becomes blatantly apparent in her ennobling of her imagination poetics. And her fondness for the lyric genre has already been touched upon. This fondness led her to use the first-person lyric format in "To Maecenas," "An Hymn to Humanity," "Elegy on Leaving ——," and particularly in her "Long Poem," among many other poems.

When we gather together these suggestions of romanticism with the others we have examined in detail—her penchant for human rights; her struggle for religious freedom; her close use of nature; her analysis of imagination as a way of knowing something new; her expression of an individual quest for a passionate individualism; her analysis of the unconscious as an instrument for poetic creativity; her determination to achieve order in a disordered, usually hostile world; and her advancement of women's rights—all these characteristics provide ample testimony that Wheatley's work strikingly parallels and even substantially prefigures the many characteristics that together identify the several British and Continental romanticisms. I submit, given the evidence assembled, that we should begin to think of this brilliant artist, perhaps a completely unexpected phenomenon in Early America, as a late-eighteenth-century romantic.

Chapter 4

After Wheatley: In England, France, and Germany, Excluding Kant

Having brought forward a formidable account of Phillis Wheatley's numerous romantic characteristics, perhaps now we have gained new insight into what it was that appealed to such persons as Thomas Clarkson and Gilbert Imlay in the English-speaking world and Johann Blumenbach and Henri Grégoire on the Continent. While none of these writers may themselves be considered to have been romantics, each was known and read by contemporaries who were or were becoming romantics. What I am trying to suggest is that not only the abolition of slavery motivated these thinkers to quote Wheatley's poems; indeed, what Wheatley actually said—that is, the content of her work, especially that of her "Long Poem"—would have easily been accepted within the flow of thought that yielded the romantic movement. In this chapter, we take up the British, French, and German fascination with Wheatley. While Wheatley's correspondence of thought to Immanuel Kant deserves close consideration, requiring a brief chapter, her connections to Coleridge prove to be far more substantial, hence demanding a more detailed analysis following the brief chapter on Kant.

The overriding appeal of Wheatley's imagination poetics to the creators of, and to those associated with, the romantic movement resided assuredly in her application of imagination as a means to address the crises of culture besetting not only her own predicament, but in addition the several cultural crises explicitly present in America and Europe. To be sure, perhaps the most readily apparent among these crises of culture is the practice of the dreaded institution, slavery. Wheatley's concerns also move, nonetheless, into the realms of women's rights, of America's quest for political independence (Wheatley was ever a steady patriot), and, probably surprisingly, of religious freedom as opposed to subscription to any dogma.

While we have touched on Wheatley's politics and support of women's rights in other venues, we need now to underscore her advancement of antislavery sentiments and religious freedom. The title of her single published volume, *Poems on Various Subjects, Religious and Moral,* highlights Wheatley's concern for moral behavior, this concern most keenly projected by the lack of morality that fosters slavery. Her use of the adjective, "Religious," suggests, moreover, that her religious concerns may prove to be as innocuous as her moral preoccupations appear to be. Of course, the operative verb relating both to "Moral" and "Religious" is *appear*. Certainly in Wheatley's case her subjects treat far deeper matters than the overwhelming majority of her readers could have suspected. As we have seen, her moral argument settles on freedom, for herself and for her Black brothers and sisters, and her ostensible endorsement of Christianity masks her attempt to use her religious consciousness to bridge the gap between her idea of God and the secular world. So in a real sense we revisit the realm of freedom, here for the freedom simply to be herself.

Because Wheatley's construction of heterocosms in "On Imagination" is so crucial to our understanding of how she used imagination to escape the world of slavery and to discover her religious freedom, some additional points of emphasis regarding this heterocosm phenomenon are in order. Peter Otto, among others, asserts that, when speaking of the several elements which characterize the romantic understanding of imagination, "crucial to these connections is the ability of the imagination to create a heterocosm or alternate world" (553). Francis Gallaway, in *Reason, Rule, and Revolt in English Classicism,* suggests that the creation of heterocosms signals the birth of romanticism when the emotional response of an individual seeks "to evolve a world-view satisfactory to the yearning heart" (347), closely related to Wheatley's yearning for a world without slavery but one with religious tolerance.

An instructive way to read "On Recollection" and "Thoughts on the Works of Providence," the first two parts of her "Long Poem," is to view these poems as preliminary to her rendering of the two heterocosms in "On Imagination." In "On Recollection," for example, the poet appears to be fascinated by "nocturnal visions" that pour into the poet's mind, "The ample treasure of her secret [unconscious] stores" (62). By the time of "Thoughts," Wheatley seizes upon the subject of sleep and dreams with real relish: "Say what is sleep? And dreams and how passing strange? / When action ceases, and ideas range / Licentious and unbounded o'er the plains?" (47). Wheatley's heterocosms in

"On Imagination" serve, then, as responses to the queries she has made in "Thoughts," so once again we find that the pieces of Wheatley's "Long Poem" are virtually inseparable. Peter Otto claims that to Keats the imagination functions as a vehicle of knowledge (as in a treasure trove of images) "Residing at a level too deep to be scrutinized by the conscious mind" (553). Perhaps we would do well, then, to understand Wheatley's heterocosms to be operational on just such a deep plain.

As we saw in *Phillis Wheatley's Poetics of Liberation,* at least two among Wheatley's contemporaries found her lack of Christianity certainly problematic. For Jupiter Hammon, who has the distinction of publishing the first poem by an African American (in 1760), Wheatley struck him as far too dependent on classicism at the expense of Christian issues; Richard Cary, one of the signers of Wheatley's "Letter of Attestation," assures the Countess of Huntingdon, Selina Hastings, and financial backer of the 1773 *Poems,* in a letter of introduction for Wheatley's projected encounter with the Countess (which actually never took place), that he was certain that her poems would display less classicism and more Christianity, as she continued to become more evangelical. Surely Cary's hope would have been dashed by the clever way Wheatley "handled" the Christian philanthropist John Thornton, when she refused to allow herself to be caught up in an evangelical adventure into Africa. Perhaps needless to say, her poems never realized the evangelicalism Cary promised the Countess. The salient observation to be made at this juncture is, nevertheless, that Wheatley's disposition toward antislavery and toward a refusal to insist on a dogmatic religious approach contributed to her European readers' interest in her work.

Wheatley promotes in her oeuvre, then, human rights for displaced Africans and for women's equality, and political and religious freedom for everyone. John Whale, in his daringly provocative *Imagination under Pressure, 1789–1832: Aesthetics, Politics and Utility,* calls this sort of movement against the status quo, when such movement is determined by a stubborn application of a creative imagination, "a means of articulating resistance" (11). Wheatley's resistance to unenlightened social values could not but have captured the attention of the Europeans as some were becoming romantics.

The British fascination with Wheatley, of course, begins with her London visit from June 17 to July 26, 1773 (see "Chronology" 123–24) and with her receipt of at least nine reviews of her *Poems,* which Archibald Bell published in early September, after her departure. The following year Hannah Moore (the Brit) mentioned Phillis Wheatley in a letter to Frances Reynolds, sister to Sir Joshua Reynolds (Bristol, September 10, 1774), wherein Moore claims to have seen a recent poem in which the author compares her to Phillis Wheatley. She adds that the comparison may go beyond the written word, for she thinks the author of the poem makes a play on Moore's dark complexion as recalling the Black woman poet. Doubtless, similar episodes of interest in Wheatley will be traced in subsequent years.

In 1786, Wheatley's reputation as a poet received a sort of jump start when Thomas Clarkson quotes from three of her poems in his popular *An Essay on the Slavery and Commerce of the Human Species, Particularly the African*. Clarkson, who was to become an indefatigable opponent of slavery, advances in his *Essay* the argument that a glance at these selections from the 1773 *Poems* proves this woman was hardly "designed for slavery" (Clarkson 122). Drawing for his selections from her hymns "To the Morning" and "Evening" and from "On Imagination," Clarkson also quotes entire the "Letter of Attestation" supposedly ascertaining the authenticity of the author's poems constituting the 1773 volume (as if she needed authentication). The fourteen lines Clarkson takes from "On Imagination" include the four-line stanza describing "the roving fancy," along with the more significant ten-line stanza beginning with the arresting line, "*Imagination!* who can sing thy force[?]" (121–22).

A great deal of the impact that Clarkson's quotations from Wheatley exercised among the British romantics and, as we will soon see, abroad, may be attributable to the fact that virtually all the British intellectual and literary world read this inflammatory work. Wordsworth owned a copy, surely noticed by Coleridge, and the German father of physical anthropology, Johann Blumenbach, owned a copy, which he speaks about in his 1790 *Beyträge zur Naturgeschichte* (*Contributions to Natural History*). (More appears later about this remarkable connection in the examination of the German interest.) The 1788 second printing of *Slavery and Commerce* enjoyed two further printings in America. In fact, Wordsworth came into possession of several others of Clarkson's works, hence suggesting that Wordsworth registered more than a casual interest in the slavery issue; Coleridge, who did quote from *Slavery and Commerce,* owned two additional Clarkson volumes.

The relationship among Catherine (wife) and Thomas Clarkson, Dorothy (sister) and William Wordsworth, and Coleridge became intimate. Dorothy and

Catherine established an extensive correspondence, and Richard Holmes, one of Coleridge's biographers, holds that Catherine and Thomas helped Coleridge "to battle against opium addiction" (Holmes 366). Wordsworth and Coleridge first met Clarkson and his wife on their first Lake District tour, this occasion taking place on November 17, 1799, when both poets stayed with the Clarksons for the night. About Clarkson, Coleridge wrote in an 1809 missive that he was "the moral Steam-Engine" of the abolition quest (Wilson 140).

Soon after striking up an acquaintance with the Clarksons, the Wordsworths and the Coleridges relocated in the Lake District, not far from Eusemere Hill, the residence of the Clarksons. Here the three families formed what some came to call the "Wordsworth circle" (Wilson 99). Given the interest Wordsworth and Coleridge both had in the abolition movement, and for Coleridge this concern became a preoccupation, it is unthinkable that these poets of *Lyrical Ballads* could have ignored Wheatley's poems as quoted by Clarkson. We should note also that the passage Clarkson took from "On Imagination" embraced the distinction Wheatley makes between fancy and imagination.

The passage Gilbert Imlay, our next author, chose from "On Imagination," which he included in his *Topographical Description of the Western Territory of North America* (London editions in 1792, 1793, and 1797), comprised all of Wheatley's first of two heterocosms, along with the "*Imagination!* who can sing thy force" stanza, but not the lines making the distinction between fancy and imagination. The fact that Imlay quotes lines different from Clarkson ascertains that he is not merely referencing Clarkson, but that he has sought out an edition of the 1773 *Poems*. This Imlay figure enjoyed a bit of infamy during his own time, for he became for a while the lover of the great intellectual and feminist Mary Wollstonecraft. He was commissioned an officer in the American Revolution as a first lieutenant, although he is called "Captain" on the title page of *Topographical Description*. His *Topographical Description*, perhaps even more popular than Clarkson's *Slavery* and enjoying a translation into German, displays a remarkable, and declared, dependence on the imaginative faculty, which suggests that he absorbed Wheatley's poetics of "On Imagination."

Topographical Description itself presents a utopian perspective of the North American continent, but its imaginative passages are heavily laden with details of geography that give the work an undeniably factual and, for the time, reliable impression of what Imlay often calls the "American empire." We should note for future reference that Imlay's *Topographical Description* proved to be of considerable interest to Coleridge and Robert Southey, as these two Cambridge University classmates plotted their "pantisocracy" project entailing the establishment of an American colony in opposition to the contemporary British government, which the two undergraduates, among many others, saw as irretrievably corrupt.

Before we examine Imlay's quite interesting take on the imagination, whose application sounds much like Wheatley's, we should trace a bit of the background Imlay acquired while in America. Having come across this information only with the fortuitous appearance of Wil Verhoeven's engrossing biography, *Gilbert Imlay: Citizen of the World* (2008), I was not prepared for what Verhoeven reveals. Verhoeven justly opens his biography with the comprehensive observation that "Imlay unwittingly acted as an interface between figures of much greater historical significance" (1). Indeed, not only did Imlay "interface" with such notables as Mary Wollstonecraft, William Wordsworth, Samuel Taylor Coleridge, and Robert Southey, but he also served as a conduit between Wheatley's "On Imagination," and, like Clarkson before him, the European romantics.

Verhoeven's biography taught me what I must say was shocking and certainly unexpected news, that Imlay briefly participated in the hated triangular trade. Verhoeven records that on March 7, 1786, Silas Talbot "sold Imlay ... a one-quarter interest in the *Industry* and her cargo" (84). As the *Industry* was unabashedly a slaver, her "cargo" was, of course, slaves. On March 9 of the same year, Talbot accepted "Imlay's promissory note for four prime slaves" (84). Given the fact that Imlay grew up on his father's New Jersey plantation, Verhoeven tells us that salves would "have been a familiar sight to Gilbert Imlay" (85). For that matter, the colony of New Jersey served the other colonies as "a transit port for slave labour" (85).

In any event, by the time of Imlay's publication in London, where he had relocated by 1792, of *Topographical Description,* his sympathies appear to have altered radically. Verhoeven, nevertheless, relates that Imlay "could never bring himself to tell" Wollstonecraft or apparently anyone else in England or France, about "his brief encounter with the triangular trade" (181). With this new knowledge, however, Imlay's impassioned attack on Thomas Jefferson for his scurrilous remarks about Blacks in general but especially for his unkind treatment of Wheatley comes as something of a surprise.

Quoting the twenty lines from "*Imagination!* who can sing thy force?" through "And nectar sparkle on the blooming rose," the salient passage that has all of Wheatley's first heterocosm, Imlay prefaces his long quotation with this ecphonesis: "Indeed, I should be glad to be informed what white upon this continent [America] has written more beautiful lines" (Imlay 229–30). Another indication that Imlay has before him a copy of the 1773 *Poems* (the lines from "On Imagination" are notably accurate) is his quote from Jefferson's *Notes* "that Terence was a slave, but not black," which is noticeably not accurate (Jefferson had "Epictetus, Terence and Phaedrus, were slaves. But they were of the race of whites"—*Notes* 191), suggesting that Imlay had more respect for Wheatley. As well, moreover, the fact that Imlay singles out Terence points directly to Wheatley's identification of Terence in her *Poems* as "African by birth." We may easily conclude, therefore, that Imlay had familiarity with all of *Poems*.

Given the fact that Imlay, on the page following the last lines of the "On Imagination" passage, accuses Jefferson of distinctly lacking an "energy of the human mind," which would/should have enabled him to access more of his own "imagination" (231) and thence to discover the value of Wheatley's achievement, gives Imlay's discussion a particularly nice touch. I should not wish to pass by the opportunity to observe how far the reputation of the imagination has traveled after Wheatley. No longer is there in Imlay's treatment of Wheatley any hint of Augustine's or Tyndale's hostility toward imagination.

This positive disposition toward imagination provocatively obtains in Imlay's text preceding his Wheatley discussion. In the "Introduction" to the volume, for example, the author registers a sort of disclaimer in the observation that his readers may sometimes fear that "the ardour of the author's imagination [calling up Wheatley's 'an intrinsic ardor prompts to write'] may exceed the just limits of truth and precision" (ix). What his readers soon receive, nevertheless, is ample evidence that Imlay's enthusiasm for his subject leads him to refer often to what some even in the 1790s would have predictably construed to be an imagination run a bit wild. In actually moving beyond the limits of expected "truth and precision," as we shall soon observe, Imlay shows his compatibility with the evolving romantics.

In the text proper, for example, Imlay describes that the remarkable vistas of the North American continent caused the early traders with Native Americans to be overwhelmed by "their enraptured imaginations" (6). Only a few pages later, the author notes that the bottom land of the Ohio evidences "as fine a body of land as the imagination can paint" (27). In both the above instances, the rhetoric is redolent of Wheatley's in her "Long Poem," in her ekphrastic "Niobe in Distress...," and in "To S.M. a Young African Painter." As well, an imagination that paints with words reminds us of Horace's *Ut picture poesis*. A few pages further, Imlay speaks of how the lands and rivers, valleys and rapids elicit "the charms of the imagination," which he holds "play upon the enraptured senses" (34–35).

Imlay appears to be summoning the subtrinity of memory (the senses, the appetites, and the imagination) as he continues his enthusiastic descriptions. At the top of the next page, he exclaims, "Heavens! What charms are there in liberty!" (36). Most suggestively, the ecstasy within these syllables precisely echoes the rhythm of Wheatley's "Imagination! who can sing thy force?" As well, the sentiments of Imlay's line parallel the temper of Wheatley's liberation poetics.

A sentence given nine pages after the "Heavens!" ecphonesis cinches the connection between imagination and the senses: "The air in this climate is pure, and the almost continual unclouded sky tends not a little to charm the senses" (45). Here Imlay conflates the earlier phrases "charms of the imagination," with a nod to "what charms are there in liberty!" and "the enraptured senses" (recall the earlier "enraptured imaginations"). The pattern that emerges from this series of juxtapositions clearly brings about a coalescence of senses, liberty, and imagination. While one may argue this pattern may well bespeak an unconscious application, I submit Imlay has responded on a deep, perhaps subliminal, level to Wheatley's "Long Poem." Imlay's task of capturing the expanse of North American geography and at the same time attempting to compose an enthusiastic, utopian promotion of European immigration invites him to rely on the expansive possibilities, not of neoclassical reason, but of romantic imagination.

Affecting an ironic posture is Imlay's assertion in his introductory remarks about Jefferson's *Notes* that "I have been ashamed, in reading Mr. Jefferson's book, to see, from one of the most enlightened and benevolent of my countrymen, the disgraceful prejudices he entertains against the unfortunate negroes" (222). Knowing about Imlay's earlier brush with the triangular trade may most immediately call into question the sincerity of Imlay's observation. As well I find it particularly ironic that, given Henry Louis Gates Jr.'s judicious exposure in several locations (but see especially his *Figures in Black*) of how contradictory to the spirit of Enlightenment was the praxis of slavery, Imlay's observation assumes the character of disingenuousness. This passage does, nevertheless, indicate a response to the crisis of culture that the triangular trade imposed on the eighteenth century.

Imlay's sympathy with "the unfortunate negroes" assuredly "looks" sincere when rendered out of context with his part ownership of the slaver *Industry*. It is worth making the point that Imlay may well have changed his mind regarding the slavery issue. In another vein, Imlay's behavior in the writing of *Topographical Description* suggests that as prominent a player in the evolving romanticism as Immanuel Kant could have, as did Imlay, revised his clearly racist position in the 1764 *Observations on the Feeling of the Beautiful and Sublime* (wherein he appears to take instruction from David Hume) by the time of the late 1780s when he takes a concerted interest in the work of the father of physical anthropology and public abolitionist Johann Blumenbach. We encounter Kant again shortly, in more detail.

Evidence that the German translation of *Topographical Description* was actually taken seriously by German readers comes in a letter from Madeleine Schweitzer to Mary Wollstonecraft; in this missive composed in the fall of 1794, Schweitzer, according to another of Wollstonecraft's biographers, "had read a German translation of Imlay's *Topographical Description* and asked Mary to send the author [Imlay] her love 'on account of what you [Imlay, once again] say about the negroes'" (Sunstein 264). Note Schweitzer's attention to "negroes." Given the availability and fame of Imlay's *Topographical Description*, it is more than mere speculation to assert that someone like Friedrich Schleiermacher, father of modern theology, may have found Imlay's citation from Wheatley's "On Imagination" palatable to his evolving theoretics of imagination expressed in, say, his 1799 *On Religion: Speeches to Its Cultured Despisers*. We will soon meet Schleiermacher again in our discussion of German connections to Wheatley.

The fact that John C. Stedman's 1796 *Narrative of a Five Year's Expedition against the Revolted Negroes of Surinam,* published first in English in London, received two German translations, compounds the likelihood that someone of Schleiermacher's curiosity may have come across Wheatley's "On Imagination"; Stedman also quotes from her poem, although the lines he selects correspond precisely to the lines from "On Imagination" chosen by Clarkson. Even though Stedman's *Narrative* does not turn up in the libraries of Wordsworth and Coleridge, we know that Coleridge consulted Stedman's *Narrative* closely enough to quote a four-line passage in a letter to Southey of September 30, 1799 (*Collected Letters* 1: 294). I should add that the lines from "On Imagination" appear in the *Narrative* only twenty pages before Coleridge's quote from Stedman. That Coleridge did not know of Wheatley's poem is now tantamount to an impossibility. Nevertheless, in the chapter on Wheatley and Coleridge, we discover irrefutable proof that Coleridge saw at least a selection from "On Imagination."

Stedman's *Narrative* gained an enormous popularity. Indeed, his *Narrative* enjoyed six English printings, as well as two German (as observed), two Dutch, one Italian, and two French printings. The "On Imagination" lines that Stedman quotes duplicate Clarkson's, except that Stedman has "And soft captivity invades the mind" instead of the correct "And soft captivity involves the mind," and "Or where describe the swiftness of thy course?" rather than "Or who describe the swiftness of thy course?" While the alterations here may reflect printers' errors, certainly greater care was taken with Wheatley's texts in Clarkson's *Slavery* and, for that matter, in Imlay's *Topographical Description*.

Stedman's remarks on Wheatley are, as well, far briefer than those given by Clarkson or Imlay. He mistakenly calls the poem "Thoughts on Imagination" but gives this positive judgment on the lines quoted: "What can be more beautiful and sublime?" (Stedman 363). We must say, nevertheless, that the popularity of Stedman's *Narrative* placed before the eyes of a plethora of Europeans the name of Phillis Wheatley, along with important lines from her most important poem.

Above we have on several occasions mentioned William Wordsworth as a possible interested party concerning Wheatley's 1773 *Poems,* but particularly we have noted how at certain times this great romantic poet encountered, if not the entire *Poems,* at least twenty lines from Wheatley's "On Imagination," in Clarkson's *Slavery* volume and/or in Stedman's *Narrative*. Because of his (and Coleridge's) great admiration for Wollstonecraft, it is tantamount to a certainty that he saw, as well, the lines Imlay quoted from "On Imagination" in his *Topographical Description*. Such a pointedly provocative analysis of the imaginative faculty as Wheatley provides, if not in the entire "On Imagination," then assuredly in the lines quoted by Clarkson, Stedman, and Imlay, could not have escaped Wordsworth's attention.

Significant interstices of thought between Wheatley and Wordsworth obtain in their emphases on the role of the passions in poetry, in their quest for the moral in a disturbing world, in their mutual appreciation of nature, in the importance to each of high pleasure, in their view of the creative act as parallel to Divine creation, and, most crucially, in their distinction between fancy and imagination. Every schoolgirl or boy knows Wordsworth's famous definition of poetry in the "Preface" to the *Lyrical Ballads* (1800) as "the spontaneous overflow of powerful feelings . . . [originating] from emotion recollected in tranquility" (Stillinger 460). As well, all students of romanticism have learned that the shaping, creative faculty that gives form to the poetic passions is imagination; Wordsworth identifies this faculty in *The Prelude* as "Reason in her most exalted mood" (Stillinger 360). What is just now becoming known is Wheatley's emphasis on imagination as the poet's creative, shaping faculty. In Wheatley's "On Imagination" the poet speaks of the imagination as the mind's "imperial queen" whose "various works" or products of the imagination, her poems, "in beauteous order stand" (65). Clearly to Wheatley, writing over a quarter century before Wordsworth, the imagination is that faculty which gives order to the poet's passions.

To Wheatley, her moment of "spontaneous overflow" comes when she writes the impassioned line, "There in one view we grasp the mighty whole" (65). Herein she records the sublime feeling, expressing the enthusiastic passions, which become known to the contemplator of the cosmic expanse of space as the "mental optics" that "Measure the skies, and range the realms above" (66). At this moment, when her mind attempts to register the incomplete pleasure evoked as her mind becomes overwhelmed by the task of understanding what it views, here anticipating Kant of the "Analytic of the Sublime," the poet discovers to herself, by use of her powerful, forceful imagination, that this very forcefulness of *her* mind enables this sublime moment. The moment is itself spontaneous and therefore temporary, provoking an overflow of emotions; she can nonetheless, as Wordsworth later instructs us, recapture this ecstatic emotion as she recollects it during the relatively tranquil process of creating the poem. The poem itself then serves as evidence of her creative ability to convey this sublime feeling by way of her own words.

As for a parallel interest in the idea of the moral, Wordsworth wrote in a letter to a faithful student of his poetry: "There is scarcely one of my Poems which does not aim to direct the attention to some moral sentiment, or to some general principle, or law of thought, or of our intellectual constitution" (*Letters,* 2: 148). In fact, Wordsworth speaks repeatedly throughout his Prefaces and Supplements of "our moral sentiments." As we have already pointed out, Wheatley's title, *Poems on Various Subjects, Religious and Moral,* clearly highlights her concern with the subject of the moral, especially when to be moral is not to permit slavery. While Wordsworth is not so particularly preoccupied with the slavery issue, certainly both poets promote in their work the virtue of moral behavior.

One can verify a preoccupation with the moral in both poets' appreciations of nature. The likely connection Wheatley and Wordsworth enjoyed in their appreciation of nature may best be traced in their reading of James Thomson's poetry. While it is widely known that, in his youth, Wordsworth was quite fond of the British Thomson (1700–1748), we need make no case for his thorough reading of Thomson's works. As no connection between Wheatley and Thomson has, to my knowledge, heretofore been made, a brief excursus into the details of this connection is now in order.

J. Logie Robertson, Thomson's principal editor, has observed that Thomson "was sincerely and healthily enamoured of nature." He adds that Thomson's "great merit lies in his restoration of nature to the domain of poetry from which it had been banished by Pope and his school" (Thomson viii). So once again we learn that the case for Wheatley's alleged slavish imitation of Pope fails to be made. Thomson's *The Seasons* (1746) was immensely popular on both sides of the Atlantic; in America, the poem enjoyed a dozen printings before 1800, the first as early as 1764. In *The Seasons* we can find several phrases which approximate phrases in Wheatley's oeuvre.

In the portion of his poem devoted to spring, for example, Thomson describes the treasures of the sun as "Luxuriant and unbounded" (6), paralleling Wheatley's similar phrasing, "Licentious and unbounded" (*Coll. Works* 47), in "Thoughts on the Works of Providence." Thomson is fond of using the word "pomp" throughout his works to embellish his conjured images, here predicting Wheatley's poems all "deck'd with pomp" (65). In a poem from Wheatley's second period of maturity (following her manumission), she speaks of the play of her "sportive fancy" (*Coll. Works* 144), while Thomson calls on his "lively fancy" (Thomson 21).

Later in "Summer," Thomson, whom many critics have identified as a romantic "at heart," appeals to the "Creative fancy" (110), expressing a conceit that Wheatley would have found palatable. In 1735, Thomson published his *Liberty*, another long poem, this one of five parts. Here he asserts that we may "in one view" (345) grasp the wonders of Roman civilization; Wheatley uses identical phrasing when, in "On Imagination," she draws her sublime moment of cosmic proportions: "There in one view we grasp the mighty whole" (*Coll. Works* 66).

But the most dramatic parallel of phrasing between Thomson and Wheatley comes in their use of the phrase "tyrannic sway." It is significant that this phrase does not appear in Shakespeare, in the King James Bible, in Milton, or in Pope. The phrase first appears in the fourth part of Thomson's *Liberty*, given to a treatment of the importance of freedom to Great Britain, a realm which eschews "tyrannic sway." Wheatley applies this phrase in her well-known celebration of the Earl of Dartmouth; as a commentary on Thomson's earlier *Liberty*, this phrase serves an ironic function. Wheatley holds that America, still in 1772 a colony of Britain, will perhaps now, with the appointment of Dartmouth, widely believed to represent a more liberal attitude toward the colonies, enjoy true freedom. For now, according to the poet, she may "but pray / Others may never feel tyrannic sway" (*Coll. Works* 74). The irony is implicit in the conditional "may"; Wheatley is already, at only eighteen, worldly wise enough to realize that freedom is ever relative to politics—and greed.

Wheatley's familiarity with Thomson's works and with his celebration of nature further align her oeuvre with that mode of mind which goes so far to explain the phenomenon of a Wordsworth. Indeed, both Wheatley and Wordsworth (and Thomson) appear ever to insist in their work that, from human interaction with nature, one may discover moral applications. Both poets' concern with the moral in nature relates directly to their quest for "high" pleasure. Each poet commits her or his work to the quest for truth and knowledge, the pursuit of which enables each to experience the highest, most noble pleasure. Defining knowledge as pleasure (Wordsworth, *Selected Poems and Prefaces* 455), Wordsworth goes on to give another definition of poetry as "the breath and finer spirit of all knowledge" (456). It follows then that poetry is itself pleasure and that from the writing (creation) of poetry one may teach oneself or others truth. This moral truth, Wordsworth is careful to explain, moreover, derives from allegiance to no single religious system (see 473–75). Wheatley also, in her mature poetry written after late 1771, reveals a similar determination, as we have found, not to give allegiance to any single religious system. The deity she seeks knowledge of in "On Imagination" dwells in an "empyreal palace" like some Olympian Zeus, and is a god of thunder, suggesting, perhaps, a blend of Zeus and Jehovah. And of course it is the imagination that enables her (and her readers) to perceive this joyous realm of grand pleasure. Indeed this same faculty has but to "command" and "joy rushes on the heart" (66–67). The sort of joy Wheatley would conjure possesses an urgency of which Wordsworth is unaware; for she wishes ardently to escape a world "Oppress'd with woes, a painful endless train" (152)—the world, of course, of slavery.

While each writer, then, understands the imagination to be that faculty which mediates between man and her or his idea of God or ultimate truth, perhaps the urgency of Wheatley's use of imagination pushed her into an early intoxication with her own power over words. This power, like that of the divinity, enables her "with new worlds [to] amaze th' unbounded soul" (66). Wordsworth writes in a similar strain when he observes "a sublime consciousness of the soul in her own mighty and almost divine powers" (Wordsworth, *Selected Poems and Prefaces* 486).

As we have observed repeatedly of Wheatley, she is preoccupied, early on, with the power(s) of memory. From "On Recollection," she moves on, in "Thoughts on the Works of Providence," to analyze the interplay of imagination and reason; recollect that it is in this poem that she makes a clear separation between the "Fancy" and her queen. What is not clear, yet, is that "*Fancy's queen*" is coterminous with the imperial queen, imagination. As "Thoughts" serves as a bridge between "On Recollection" and "On Imagination," the poet has not determined to identify the reason as the poet's reason or imagination, as she suggests in the link "thus to *Reason* (so let *Fancy* rove)" (48). By the time of "On Imagination," however, Wheatley has made the leap from subordinating fancy to reason to declaring that imagination is "leader of the mental train," that is the poet's reason. All these faculties—memory, reason, and imagination—constitute powers of her mind that enable her capacity over words to convey her deep, interior ideas.

Wordsworth expresses a similar pattern of mind in his apostrophe to imagination from book 6 of *The Prelude*. Here he exclaims:

> Imagination—here the Power so called
> Through sad incompetence of human speech—
> That awful Power rose from the Mind's abyss
> ... I was lost,
> Halted without an effort to break through;
> But to my conscious soul I now can say,
> "I recognize thy glory." (book 6, ll. 593–600)

In this state, so Wordsworth maintains, the ardent poet finds him or herself "blest in thoughts [imaginations] / That are their own perfection" (book 6, ll. 612–13). In "On Imagination," composed some forty years earlier, Wheatley intones a parallel, prefiguring moment of mind when she boldly avows that the "pow'r" of imagination traces "all thy works" (her poems) "In full perfection"; indeed, continues the enraptured poet, "At thy command joy rushes on the heart" (67).

While similarity of thought already given permits us to argue that Wheatley has more in common with the British romantics than with the neoclassicists of her era, her distinction between imagination as imperial queen and fancy as subordinate instrument of imagination still more closely aligns her poetics with Wordsworth's. Wordsworth appears to have been reluctant to separate these two faculties; in the "Preface" of 1800, he speaks of "fancy or imagination," hazarding no distinction whatever. By 1815, the year of the revised "Preface," however, Wordsworth is prepared to make a distinction. Here fancy is "capricious" and yields effects that are "surprising, playful, ludicrous, amusing, tender," and so on (Stillinger 488); this faculty Wordsworth also characterizes as "a voluntary activity in shifting the scenery of the mind" (482), sounding much like Wheatley's roving fancy; he clarifies this function when in *The Prelude* he writes of nature's "works, as they present to Fancy's choice / Apt illustrations of the moral world" (363). Wheatley speaks of fancy in similar terms as roving here and there "Till some lov'd object strikes her wand'ring eyes, / Whose silken fetters all the senses bind, / and soft captivity involves the mind" (65); this same faculty she describes as playful and sportive: "Pleas'd with the theme, see sportive fancy play" (144).

As for imagination per se, Wordsworth and Wheatley appear to be in accord. Wordsworth insists that "the Imagination is conscious of an indestructible dominion" that incites and supports "the eternal" (489). For Wheatley, there can be no doubt but that the imagination is "leader of the mental train" who bears "the scepter o'er the realms of thought." That this faculty exercises an "indestructible dominion" is illustrated by Wheatley's assertion that "In full perfection all thy works are wrought" (67). Unlike Wheatley, however, Wordsworth does not precisely distinguish fancy as an instrument in service of the imagination, one that, so says Wheatley, merely "dresses to delight the *Muse*" (68). Rather Wordsworth finally sees the fancy as also a creative faculty, one nonetheless with less capacity than imagination. To be sure, Wheatley's distinction between fancy and imagination more closely resembles Coleridge's delineation of fancy and the secondary imagination in *Biographia Literaria* (1817). We will investigate this resemblance in detail in chapter 6.

While Wheatley's and Wordsworth's motivations to create poetry offer compelling parallels, doubtless Wordsworth would have found his poetic self without hints from Phillis Wheatley. Parallels of thought do not yield indications of concrete influence. But, after all, the ascertaining of concrete influence is not our objective at this juncture. Rather, those substantial parallels do, nevertheless, amply demonstrate that Wheatley's poetic theoretics and subjects fall comfortably within the province of those of Wordsworth. Indeed, the transatlantic cultural conversation in which the works of these two poets engage suggests powerful romantic contiguities. More to the point, we must concede that Wheatley investigates the enthusiastic passions (the sublime), turning inward to express the intense pleasure available to the poet who explores her or his own individuality, celebrating salubrious nature, focusing on moral behavior reflecting the cultural crisis that ensues from a lack of morality (as in the praxis of slavery), understanding creativity in terms evoking parallels to divine creativity, and seeking to distinguish between fancy and imagination—all these processes pursued at least twenty-five years before these concerns begin to appear in Wordsworth's work.

※ ※ ※

Recognition of Wheatley's contribution to that thought which resulted in the establishment of the various European romanticisms most definitely does characterize a central desideratum of this investigation. That contribution, as we have found, assuredly emanates in great part from the international absorptive concern to bring about the abolition of slavery. In France this concern received strong stimulus from Antoine de Laplace's 1745 translation of

Aphra Behn's short novel *Oroonoko, or the Royal Slave* (1688), which according to Edward D. Seeber, in *Anti-slavery Opinion in France during the Second Half of the Eighteenth Century,* "furnished a model for much of the subsequent *littérature négrophile* in France. The immense popularity of Behn's *Oroonoko* moved the Victorian poet, Algernon Swinburne, to assert that Behn must be considered 'the first literary abolitionist . . . on record in the history of fiction'" (28).

This absorptive concern for abolition led to the publication, by 1789, in Paris of three French adaptations of Clarkson's *An Essay on the Slavery and Commerce of the Human Species,* in which Clarkson quotes selections from the morning and evening hymns (paeans) and from "On Imagination." Just so, we may immediately conclude that the name of Phillis Wheatley, along with selections from three of her poems, was certainly placed before French readers, in French (Seeber 85n55). The first mention of Wheatley in French that I have been able to locate comes down to us from no less a source than François Arouet de Voltaire, French philosophé, encyclopédiste, and author of *Candide* (among many others). In a letter to a colleague written in 1774, while he was in London (avoiding arrest by an unfavorable government), he relates that Fontenelle was mistaken when he claimed that Blacks could not write, for "*il y a actuellment une Nègresse qui fait de très-bons vers anglais*" (there is now a Negress who has made very good English verse; Seeber 57n53).

Another French writer who took an interest in Wheatley was Lecointe-Marsillac, who in *Le More-Lach* (1789) notes that the works of Wheatley (along with the slave narrative of Ignatius Sancho) offer proof of Black intelligence (Seeber 174–75). We see, then, that the name and at least some works by Wheatley were publicly spoken of among the French. The year 1789 was indeed an important one for Wheatley in France, for also in this year Joseph Lavallée came out with a novel, *Le Nègre comme il y a peu de Blancs,* translated as *The Negro Equalled by Few Europeans*. Owing much to Aphra Behn's *Oroonoko,* Lavallée's novel becomes especially important to Wheatley studies when in two American editions of an English translation, the Philadelphia printer, William W. Woodward, appends Lavallée's lengthy novel with a copy of the entire 1773 *Poems,* which he somewhat oddly calls, *Poems on Various Subjects, Religious and Entertainting,* in both his 1801 printings.

It is certainly possible that one of these Woodward printings of the 1773 *Poems* crossed the Atlantic while Henri Grégoire was working on his 1808 *De la littérature des négres,* translated by P. B. Warden in 1810 and also published in Philadelphia. As the title of the English translation indicates, *An Enquiry Concerning the Intellectual and Moral Faculties and Literature of Negroes* (1810), the faculties of Blacks were and continue to be major points of emphasis; Grégoire's method is sociological rather than anthropological. Here he finds the merits of equality of the races in the literary productions of Blacks in Latin, French, and other languages, as well as those in English. In his assessment, Phillis Wheatley's achievement in poetry is not the least successful of these literary productions.

According to his own testimony, Grégoire borrowed Johann Blumenbach's copy of the 1773 *Poems* to make his observations about Wheatley's poetry. Grégoire gives a brief, but often inaccurate biographical sketch of Wheatley's life as a slave and her efforts toward her education, although his treatment is more extensive than that of any preceding sketches (two full pages as opposed to a few lines in the others); he quotes from her poetry and reproduces three complete poems ("On the Death of J.C. an Infant," "An Hymn to the Morning," and "To the Right Honorable William Earl of Dartmouth") rather than merely a few lines. He also takes the time to refute Jefferson's unwillingness "to acknowledge the talents of negroes, even those of Phillis Wheatley" (236), as we earlier observed of Clarkson and Imlay.

But at this point, Grégoire departs from the pattern established by earlier writers who mention or quote from her poetry, his comments moving beyond simple panegyric toward a more judicious examination of her subject matter. Rather than merely displaying her work with a minimum of enthusiastic comment, he observes that her "Ode to Maecenas," which opens the 1773 volume, shows a familiarity with Horace. He comments further upon this poem that, "It is not without merit; but we hasten to subjects more worthy of her muse" (238). This French abolitionist remarks as his final evaluation of Wheatley's poetry, "Almost all her poetical productions have a religious or moral cast—all breathe a soft and sentimental melancholy" (238). Grégoire recognizes Wheatley's achievement in verse, but unlike most writers before him, he does not find her poems to be beautiful. He does, however, attempt to defend her poetry on the basis of its content—not merely because it is the product of a Black woman. His treatment of her more closely approaches a balanced critical assessment than those of previous readers. Grégoire was probably the first earnest apologist for Wheatley's poetry, one who based his defense upon an examination of the poems themselves.

While the French connection to Wheatley is less dramatic than that which may be shown to exist between her and the British or between her and the Germans (as we are about to see), the French connection is, nonetheless, worthy of our attention. Indeed, the French interest in her work tells us how far her texts and name traveled during this era, hence compounding the interfacing role she and her poems played in the developing Continental romanticisms. Surely other investigators after me will discover still more French connections.

* * *

The German experience of Wheatley's texts certainly moves far beyond the French interest. Indeed, the compatibility of her imagination poetics strikingly predicts the kind of enthusiasm toward imagination Friedrich Schleiermacher displays in his 1799 *On Religion: Speeches to Its Cultured Despisers*. This most learned and sophisticated man and father of modern theology declared in the "Second Speech" of five that "By imagination I do not mean anything subordinate or confused, but the highest and most original faculty in man." Schleiermacher even goes so far as to maintain that "All else in the human mind is simply reflection upon it" (*Speeches* 98). James Engell, whose treatment of the German interest in the creative imagination approaches masterful coverage, points out that for Schleiermacher, the artist (poet) "is 'a true priest of the Highest' [Divinity] who 'presents the heavenly and the eternal'" (Engell, 238).

Later in his systematic theology, known as *The Christian Faith* (1821–1822), Schleiermacher holds that "The poetic expression is always based originally upon a moment of exaltation which has come purely from within a moment of enthusiasm or inspiration" (1: 78). This theologian then proceeds to declare, "For when anyone finds himself in a state of unusually exalted religious self-consciousness, he will feel himself called to poetic description" (1: 79). Schleiermacher's emphases on feeling, emotion, and exaltation actually provide a closely accurate description of Phillis Wheatley's approach to the composing process. This theologian's melding of the secular office of creating poetry with unmistakable religious feeling bespeaks the kind of deep-seated, sometimes almost unconscious response that characterizes the writings of such serious poets as Wheatley, Wordsworth, Shelley, and Keats.

This brief excursus into Schleiermacher's regard for the creative imagination serves as a preamble to our investigation of the recurrence of Wheatley's salient texts within that thought which begins to describe the growth of German romanticism. One additional point regarding Schleiermacher we must not fail to make is that, at least as early as 1807, Coleridge owned one of Schleiermacher's books and later acquired two others. Andrew Bowie, in his *Aesthetics and Subjectivity: From Kant to Nietzsche,* says of Schleiermacher, "Like the early Romantics, with whom he had close, but often critical contact, [he] does not believe in philosophy's ability to articulate the Absolute." Rather for Schleiermacher, art functions "as the product of human freedom which is the object of 'aesthetics'" (Bowie 149). As we have observed of Phillis Wheatley's thought, human freedom is above all other issues her central concern.

The German abolitionist and father of physical anthropology, Johann Friederich Blumenbach, put forward the name and poetry of Phillis Wheatley in his 1790 *Contributions to Natural History.* Acknowledging that he possessed English, Dutch, and Latin poems by several Black writers, he singles out the poems of "Phillis Wheatley of Boston, who is justly famous for them." In a footnote to this passage, he elaborates that Wheatley's 1773 *Poems,* noting that it was available in an octavo volume, is "A collection which scarcely any one who has any taste for poetry could read without pleasure." To this observation he then adds that "the worthy Clarkson," in his *On the Slavery and Commerce of the Human Species,* has placed "Some particularly beautiful selections" (Blumenbach, 310). So we see that Wheatley's *Poems* and Clarkson's volume with lines from the morning and evening hymns, and from "On Imagination," were not merely owned by a prominent German intellectual but that this generous man sought actively to promote Wheatley's *Poems* among the German-speaking peoples.

The French Grégoire's request to borrow Blumenbach's copy of the 1773 *Poems* certainly attests the extent to which Blumenbach popularized the name and work of Phillis Wheatley. For that matter, Blumenbach's shepherding of Wheatley's contribution necessitates that we investigate both Blumenbach's role in helping to promote her texts certainly in Germany, and, as we shall learn in chapter 6, his effort to recommend her cause to the developing aesthetic consciousness of a young man with abolitionist leanings, Samuel Taylor Coleridge. Nevertheless, we now turn our attention to Wheatley and Kant.

Chapter 5

Kant and Wheatley

With so much to-do in Germany attending Wheatley's poetry, it becomes possible that even an unlikely person such as Immanuel Kant may have come across either her name or her poems. I have, since the days of my dissertation, been fascinated by the numerous proximations of thought and application of a theoretics of imagination that obtain between these two. We must, nevertheless, proceed here with considerable caution; as one of my interested colleagues has expounded, "Kant she ain't!" But I hastily add that my contention has never been to make such a reckless claim. All I am attempting to establish is, as above, the demonstrable evidence that Wheatley's salient texts (those most heavily laden with romantic qualities) did, in point of fact, participate substantially in the flow of thought that evolved into romanticism. As I understand Kant's contribution to this flow of thought that yielded the romantic movement, his participation was absolutely necessary, simply because his "Analytic of the Sublime" section (almost an afterthought) in *The Critique of Judgment* treated the theoretics of the enthusiastic passions or the feeling of the sublime, for the first time, in a systematic manner, thereby legitimating the sublime as an aesthetic pleasure. (It should be acknowledged that Kant was not trying to sanction the enthusiastic passions at all social levels, only as the sublime interfaced with aesthetics.)

As many, but not all, find Kant to be the father of modern philosophy, we need to step back a bit and prepare a context in which to see how a figure like Wheatley could have come to his attention. Kant's fondness for English literary productions has long been known, for the now classic eleventh edition of *Encyclopedia Britannica* (1910–11) informs its readers that Kant was "well versed in English literature" (15: 663). In a recent biography of Kant, entitled simply *Kant: A Biography,* Manfred Kuehn assures us that Kant:

> not only read and appreciated the current German, French, and English authors, but he tried to put their theories into praxis. Furthermore, there was a definite literary flavor to his life. He strove to be a man of letters, not just a scholar, and that set him apart from most of his colleagues at the university [the University of Konigsberg]. (134)

I leave it to others to conclude whether or not Kant "tried to put" Phillis Wheatley's theoretics of imagination "into praxis." Perhaps it was the knowledge among his colleagues that Kant "strove to be a man of letters" which led authorities at the university to offer Kant a professorship of poetry in the year 1764, a position that Kant declined.

This year, 1764, was nevertheless an important one intellectually for Kant, for his *Observations on the Feeling of the Beautiful and Sublime* was published at this time, displaying his interest in aesthetics but also expressing his lifelong inquiry regarding the races. It is certainly so, and painful to recall, that Kant shows in this work that, in 1764, he subscribes to Hume's notion that "The Negroes of Africa have by nature no feeling that rises above the trifling" (*Observations* 110). Henry Louis Gates Jr., in his important *Figures in Black*, correctly expresses outrage for this so-called enlightened perspective (and others like it in Jefferson, and in the next century, Hegel). For Kant's time, however, this sort of thinking, unacceptable to those of us today, was not typically, however regrettably, out of line. As Arthur O. Lovejoy instructs us in his *Great Chain of Being*, Blacks were in the great scheme of things not then believed to be quite human. I point out these facts, certainly *not* to defend Kant, Hume, Jefferson, Hegel, and their sort, but to place their positions within a historical context.

At the very least, Kant registers in 1764 a curiosity about Africans. In 1775 Kant announced a series of lectures treating "Of the Different Human Races" (Kuehn xvii). I am assuredly not trying to argue that somehow Kant ever became an abolitionist, although his career was certainly punctuated by a continuing interest in issues of race. At this juncture it appears sensible to introduce into our discourse the friendship between Kant and Joseph Green, an English expatriate merchant who was to become Kant's closest friend. Kuehn asserts that their relationship probably "dates back to the summer of 1765" (155). "This much is sure," holds Kuehn, "that by 1766 they were close friends;

and at least from that time on Kant was a constant and very regular visitor at Green's house" (155).

Recall that John Wheatley was a prosperous Boston merchant who owned two frigates. As well, when in London, Wheatley encountered Brook Watson, a London merchant who had visited New England and the Caribbean. Watson gave Wheatley a folio edition of Milton's *Paradise Lost* (now at Harvard's Houghton); the following year Watson was elected Lord Mayor of London. So it is plausible that this collect of merchants, including Green's expatriate merchant partner, Robert Motherby—who also became Kant's friend and whom Kant advised regarding the education of his sons—could have shown an interest in the phenomenal Phillis Wheatley. As the transatlantic merchant community was a somewhat selective one, we should probably expect that all these men at least knew of one another. Green's known preference for English authors undoubtedly exercised an influence, says Kuehn, on Kant's own study of British authors (Kuehn 156).

Kuehn postulates that the two men, Green and Kant, had a dispute about the Stamp Act of 1765; we observe that, as Kuehn's information derives from letters between the two men, Kant showed a concerted interest in the American colonies only shortly after publication of his *Observations on the Feeling of the Beautiful and Sublime*. The riots that ensued following the enactment of the Stamp Act of 1765 made international news. The fact that Wheatley wrote a celebratory response to the repeal of the Stamp Act and published this poem in her 1773 *Poems* would have surely, had they come across it, arrested their attention.

To return to Kant per se, John H. Zammito, in *The Genesis of Kant's Critique of Judgment*, notes that Kant's interest in empirical anthropology evolved "out of travelers' narratives of faraway places and 'primitive' [a misperception during Kant's century] races" (191–92). We would expect then that such tracts as Michel Adanson's *A Voyage to Senegal, the Isle of Goree, and the River Gambia* (1759), Anthony Benezet's *Some Historical Account of Guinea... with an Inquiry into the Rise and Profess of the Slave Trade* (1762), and several others, all of which were widely distributed, would have been readily available to Kant. Certainly Kant's concern for racial theoretics was piqued by his unfavorable reviews of Johann Herder's *Ideen zur Philosophie der Geschichte der Menscheit* which appeared in the mid-1780s. In the *Ideen,* Herder, a former pupil of Kant, attempted to map out a theoretics for the races. The second volume of two, so Zammito tells us, "dealt with physical anthropology and race theory, scientific topics of direct relevance to Kant's teleology essay," which closes *The Critique of Judgment;* in this teleology section Kant singles out Blumenbach by name: "Herr Hofrat Blumenbach" (Zammito 274).

The earlier appearance of Blumenbach's *On the Natural Variety of Mankind* in 1775, the year of Kant's lectures on the different races, could not but have impacted Kant's thinking about the races and as well helped to prepare him to review Herder's *Ideen*. This publication also marks Kant's introduction to Blumenbach, whose subsequent revised editions and new works, such as his *Institutions of Physiology,* first published in 1786, continued to provoke Kant's curiosity. We should not forget to point out that these and other works by Blumenbach became of considerable interest to Coleridge. In a letter of March 25, 1790, Kant instructed his publisher of *The Critique of Judgment* to send Blumenbach (and several others) a copy of the newly printed *Critique*. By August 5, 1790, Kant felt moved to write Blumenbach himself; herein he declares that "I have found much instruction in your writings, but the latest of them has a close relationship to the ideas that preoccupy me" (*Correspondence* 354).

Kant is referring in this case to Blumenbach's *Contributions to Natural History,* which had just come out; Blumenbach mentions in this work Wheatley's *Poems* and Clarkson's *On the Slavery and Commerce*. I am herein positing that Kant had already seen both Wheatley and Clarkson. Even following the death of his dear friend, Joseph Green, in 1786, Kant continued to pursue his interest in British literature and in questions of race, but now through his friendship with Robert Motherby, who inherited the firm of Green and Motherby. As Clarkson's *Slavery and Commerce* caused quite a sensation, hence launching Clarkson's abolitionist career, we may plausibly conclude that Kant saw Clarkson's selections from the morning and evening hymns, and from "On Imagination," which contains, as do Imlay's and Stedman's quotes from this poem, the line "Imagination! who can sing thy force?"

Before we get into an examination of Kant's *Critique* and Wheatley's imagination poetics, we need to make one further point. In his "Biographical Sketches" for his edition of Kant's *Correspondence* in which he details information about those who wrote Kant or received missives from him, Arnulf Zweig is careful to state that Kant, like Blumenbach, "saw all races as entitled to equal rights and privileges" (Kant, *Correspondence* 566). As we learned earlier, Mary Wollstonecraft's lover, Gilbert Imlay, at an earlier time in his illustrious career had part ownership in a slaver and had even purchased slaves. Yet this former lieutenant in the American Revolution comes across in his later *Topographical Description* as a staunch antislavery advocate, using Wheatley as proof that Blacks were not made to be slaves. To be sure, Kant never owned slaves or a slaver, so can we not entertain the possibility that this man, so concerned with moral behavior, later mollified his essentially negative position in the 1764 *Observations,* this work appearing, we should note, almost two years before Kant befriended the British merchant Joseph Green?

With so much demonstrated evidence that Kant was remarkably concerned with issues related to race theory and given the broad availability of salient texts by Phillis Wheatley, the notion that Kant may have come across the name and work of this significant and popular poet becomes not so remote. In any case, the parallels of thought between Kant and Wheatley prove to be compelling. In Kantian epistemology, the imagination serves as a condition of all possible knowledge because of its capacity to synthesize the raw contents of the mind. For Wheatley the force of imagination ennobles knowledge of the Divine; or as she has it, on the wings of imagination "we"—she and her understanding readers—may soar "through air to find the bright abode ... of the thundr'ing God" (66). As well, here as in Kant, Wheatley clearly articulates a description of imagination at free play, which for both philosopher and poet constitutes the condition of art.

This sort of mental process, so apparent in Kant's *Critique of Judgment,* goes a long way toward an explication of Wheatley's "Long Poem." We should add that this kind of mental activity, in both, points toward romanticism. In this activity of mind, imagination often provides access to knowledge *and* truth, just as this action of mind holds art to be of supreme value. As we have already observed, such a grasp of imagination and art readily obtains in significant works by Friedrich Schleiermacher.

Among the more specific parallels that occur between Wheatley and Kant are consideration of the imaginative faculty as mediator between sensibility (the lower faculty of memory, including the subtrinity of the senses, the appetites, and imagination, although this last member of the three begins immediately to show signs of definite elevation) and understanding; elevation of imagination to a high level amid the cognitive powers; the imagination touted as a productive faculty of creativity; a more detailed examination of imagination as a means toward new knowledge; imagination as instrumental in provoking an intuitive reordering of aesthetic elements, hence resulting in a grasp of new rules created by the artist conducive toward the making of her or his art; and use of imagination to convey to the artist and her or his audience an individual/personal idea of the Divinity.

Two particularly helpful recent volumes that argue for a more significant emphasis on the centrality of imagination to Kant's aesthetic theoretics are Sarah Gibbons' *Kant's Theory of Imagination: Bridging Gaps in Judgment and Experience* and Jane Kneller's *Kant and the Power of Imagination*. While Gibbons argues that imagination bridges the gaps between experience and cognition, Kneller focuses on imagination as a power of creativity in Kant's aesthetics. I wish to make clear that both Gibbons and Kneller challenge traditional, dare I say conventional, interpretations of Kant's theoretics that tend to deemphasize the role of imagination. I should like to add as well that, as so much of the content of this monograph flies fully in the face of convention, I consider myself to be in good company.

In chapter 2, we found that Joseph Seccombe had extolled imagination as an effective, powerful faculty which, however, "can never be serviceable without the Understanding" (*Some Occasional Thoughts,* 9). If imagination is "serviceable" to the understanding, then it follows that imagination must mediate between the senses/appetites and the understanding. Charron, from whom Seccombe quotes (9), had earlier asserted that the imagination, "though the Man be asleep," represents the recollection of the senses so well and in "so strong, so lively [a way], that the Imagination does the very same to the Understanding now, which the Object it self did, by the first and freshest Impression heretofore" (*De la sagesse,* Stanhope trans. 109). Kneller points out that, in the second, 1787 edition of the *Critique of Pure Reason,* "Kant defines the imagination as 'the faculty of presenting in intuition an object that is *not itself present*'" (99; Kant's three critiques are the 1781 *Critique of Pure Reason,* the 1788 *Critique of Practical Reason,* and the 1790 *Critique of Judgment*). I should like to suggest that Seccombe, Charron, and Kant appear to be on the same page regarding their respective representations of this particular function of imagination.

Wheatley, who probably did know of Seccombe and therefore of Charron, comes to a quite similar grasp of imagination when she describes in "On Recollection" the "pomp of images display'd" during "our nocturnal visions" (62). Wheatley, however, when she makes a distinction between fancy and imagination in "Thoughts" and "On Imagination"—both later poems than "Recollection"—moves a few steps beyond Charron, Seccombe, and even Kant (in the second edition of *Pure Reason*) as she assigns a much higher role to imagination per se than any of these three thinkers, thereby relegating fancy to a subordinating function in service to imagination.

By the time of the *Critique of Judgment*, however, we find Kant to have progressed in his description of imagination. According to Kneller, Kant's granting to imagination a productive, creative function in the third, 1790 *Critique* indicates an advance of sorts in Kant's thought toward consideration of imagination to be "capable of transforming nature and exhibiting human ideals in concrete form" (14). This new understanding, says Kneller, brings about in Kant an "elevation of the function of imagination to the status of creative faculty" (11). Kneller continues by declaring that this new raising up of imagination "opens the way for a philosophical turn towards viewing imagination as the main player on the human mental stage" (4). But notice here that Kneller justly holds that Kant's new grasp of imagination's creative function merely "turns towards" the idea that imagination may serve as "main player." Wheatley has, in "On Imagination," already elevated imagination, in 1773, to "leader of the mental train."

In a letter of January 3, 1791, written within a year of the third *Critique*'s publication, Kant speaks of the "productive power of the imagination" (*Correspondence* 372). A bit later, during the summer of 1792, Kant writes to a Russian prince, Alexander von Beloselsky, who was, in addition to serving as an envoy in Dresden, a poet, that the union of the powers of judgment and reason "with the power of imagination . . . constitutes genius" (*Correspondence* 418). Wheatley assuredly demonstrates that, in her elevation of imagination to the poet's reason, she has, however wittingly or unwittingly, enrolled herself in the rare company of those possessing genius.

Kant, in this same letter to the Russian prince, extends his discussion of genius from the third *Critique* by remarking that "by uniting of sensibility with the higher powers" we "discover, by means of the imagination . . . what serves as a rule without being guided by rules." Such a grasp of how the mind of the artistic genius functions leads us to conclude that the "sphere of genius . . . really cannot be counted as part of the mere understanding"

(*Correspondence* 419). In other words, the mind of genius taps into another power of mind beyond the understanding; this power is, of course, that of the imagination. Note here that Kant is drawing on his discussion from the third *Critique* that the artist of genius, in intuition, exhibits new rules rather than "following recognized rules." The imagination itself, then, according to Gibbons, "creates and exhibits order and coherence in intuition, which . . . makes concept-application or rule-following possible" (110). But I would add that this "rule-following" presupposes that the artist shapes the text, say in the writing of a poem, according to her own rules. Wheatley, therefore, speaks eloquently of imagination's power to create a "beauteous order" when there is none—that is, when human beings enslave their fellow beings.

So Wheatley's "beauteous order" results from her construction of her own rules, a creative engagement that would not have appeared inapposite to Kant in his own grasp of aesthetic creativity. As for finding her own rules, Wheatley would have had to move no further than her own mind's determination to create an orderly world, although she may have received ample encouragement from the singing master and composer, William Billings. This determination to discover to herself her own rules for composition—say, especially, in her choice of subject matter—points directly toward Wheatley's personal turn inward, which characterizes the first period of her mature career as a poet.

This inward turn that describes Wheatley's movement of mind during the first period of her poetic maturity points directly toward Wheatley's realization of imagination as enabler of free play within the soul; as well, this free play enabled by imagination prefigures Kant's insistence that, as articulated by Sarah Gibbons, "fine art arouses pleasure by producing," as a response to art, "the free play of imagination and understanding that expresses purposiveness without a purpose" (106). The perception of "purposiveness without purpose" brings Kant to assert that, so remarks Gibbons, "the artist herself must not be constrained by rules that would hinder the free play of the faculties" (106). I heartily approve of Gibbons's use of the feminine reflexive pronoun here, as it can be construed precisely to relate to Wheatley.

This rehearsal of the necessity for free play as a register of the artist's capacity to make her own rules fully accords with Wheatley's determination to employ an exercise of mind that moves "Licentious and unbounded" (47). As a manifestation of freedom, offered in the middle of her "Thoughts on the Works of Providence," Wheatley, in Kant's words, concludes that "nature"—

as we have suggested, wherein nature affects a sort of Wordsworthian pantheism—"by the medium of genius, does not prescribe rules to science but to art" (*Critique of Judgment* 151).

Building on this premise, Kant later tells us that "The imagination (as a productive faculty of cognition) is very powerful in creating another nature, as it were, out of the material nature gives it" (*Critique of Judgment* 157). Has not Kant precisely recorded Wheatley's use of natural creation in her "Thoughts and Works of Providence" to lead her to a new grasp of how her "mental pow'rs" (48) have directed her to feel the impact of her idea of "Resistless beauty" (49)?

Such an irresistible beauty accords remarkably with what Kant later insists indicates what is morally good: "Now I say the beautiful is the symbol of the morally good" (*Critique of Judgment,* 198). Perhaps this recognition of "Resistless beauty" epitomizes for Wheatley her own understanding of the "Moral" in her title, *Poems on Various Occasions, Religious and Moral.* Freedom for Wheatley allows her to use her productive imagination to discover an idea of the moral, whose absolute beauty, of course, tolerates no enslavement.

We should be remiss if we did not add that such artistic activity as spoken of by both Wheatley and Kant represents an extension of knowledge; as Gibbons notes of Kant, "Imagination offers a wealth of material to thought which is not knowable in terms of natural science" (113). Such new insight into the world of knowledge results in new knowledge, enabling Wheatley, for example, to propose her two heterocosms in "On Imagination." These excellent expressions of the power of interior thought produce what De Quincey has called a literature of power, in contradistinction to a literature of knowledge, which instructs merely. Literature of knowledge easily relates to Kant's idea of "prescribing rules to science"; literature of power manifests to De Quincey "deep sympathy with truth" (Abrams and Stillinger 548).

As well, De Quincey holds that this literature of power employs as its "very *first* step in power . . . flight" of the mind, striving toward "an ascending movement into another element where earth is forgotten" (548). Surely Wheatley invites her readers into such a flight toward truth when she challenges our "mental optics" to "range the realms above" in order to "grasp the mighty whole" (66). Wheatley's celebration here of the noumenal phenomenon of total space so very closely captures Kant's later ideas in his "Analytic of the Sublime" of the mind's incomplete capacity to grasp absolute space (resulting in an incomplete pleasure).

Here, Wheatley also embraces Kant's argument, so states Kneller of Kant, that imagination is fully "capable of transforming nature and exhibiting human ideals in concrete form" (14). To be sure, in Wheatley's case the poet has used her art—her genius, if you will—to concretize her ideal of nature within her poem, her "beauteous order" of words.

What gives most concrete form to her romantic disposition, nevertheless, is her ability to use her powerful imagination to link her "inner world of freedom and the outer world of nature" (Kneller, 17) within her two heterocosms. Indeed, in the first we witness the breaking of iron chains that spontaneously yields the rebellious world of Flora and Sylvanus, where "Show'rs may descend, / And dews their gems disclose, / And nectar sparkle on the blooming rose" (66–67). In her second created, alternative world of her beloved Mother's celestial expanse, she enrolls herself in the royal house of Memnon. As we have already observed, these two alternative worlds are bereft of slavery, hence depicting realms of the intensely moral.

We have uncovered several—perhaps unlikely, but nonetheless definite—contiguities of thought between Phillis Wheatley and Immanuel Kant, and these intellectual connections, we must point out, are anything but casual. Wheatley constructs an aesthetics wherein imagination enables the mind to act within an interior realm of free play, leading of course to concrete expressions of freedom. This new world of freedom, I would venture, for both poet and philosopher would exclude slavery. In this complex process, both poet and philosopher discover new knowledge, which for both gives them new insight into the world of the deity. As Gibbons puts it, but I add Wheatley, both demonstrate how imagination provides "the human model of divine knowing" (Gibbons, vii).

While such intellectual connections are indeed arresting, I offer one final connection, this one acting to unify all the others. Most curious, the word Kant prefers for "imagination" is, in German, *Einbildungskraft,* which Arnulf Zweig, translator and editor of Kant's *Correspondence,* carefully glosses as made up (as a compound) of *Einbildung* (imagination) and *Kraft* (power or force) (*Correspondence* 619–30; for a reliable history of *Einbildungskraft,* see *Biographia Literaria* 168n–170n). Uncannily, Wheatley's most striking single line, which appears in Clarkson, Imlay, Stedman, and of course in the 1773 *Poems,* is "Imagination! who can sing thy force?" For if the poet herself sings the force of imagination, surely she must combine the two into a single concept as imagination/force. Wheatley penned this line in 1773, anticipating Kant by some seventeen years. Finally, however, we must observe that, while Kant's grasp of imagination is constrained to the function of mediator, Wheatley has already elevated imagination to supreme faculty of the human mind, her courage here recalling Bruno and prefiguring Samuel Taylor Coleridge's promotion of this human faculty.

Chapter 6

Wheatley and Coleridge

When Wheatley subordinated fancy to imagination, she broke the rules of aesthetic decorum. But as James Engell points out, Dugald Stewart is the one who receives the credit for this sort of separation between fancy and imagination, as described in Stewart's 1792 *Elements of the Philosophy of the Human Mind* (see Engell 175–76 and 187–88). Note, however, that Stewart's insight was not registered until nineteen years after Wheatley's *Poems*. Engell is also careful to express that "Coleridge thought highly of Stewart and without doubt had read" those passages describing a distinction between fancy and imagination (175–76). Regrettably, Engell ignores any possibility that Coleridge may have encountered Wheatley's prior distinction. I submit that even Stewart may well have taken the hint for separating the offices of fancy and imagination from Wheatley's "On Imagination," either as given in *Poems* or as reproduced in Clarkson's 1786 *Slavery and Commerce.*

If Wheatley's subordination of fancy to imagination broke the rules of expected artistic behavior, then surely her elevation of imagination to supreme faculty of the human mind manifested, in 1773, outright rebellion. Jane Kneller argues in *Kant and the Power of Imagination* that Kant presents in the *Critique of Judgment* an analysis of imagination that "opens the way for a philosophical turn towards viewing imagination as the main player on the human mental stage" (4). As she acknowledges, however, for Kant imagination's role remains that of "a central mediating faculty" (4). Perhaps Kant's favorable turn of mind toward imagination was reinforced by Wheatley's enthusiasm in "On Imagination." Wheatley, of course, extols imagination as so powerful that it enacts the mind's highest essence. The African American poet moves in her aesthetics of imagination far beyond viewing this faculty as merely a mediator.

Phillis Wheatley, as I have observed before, was very likely forced to explore her poetics as a means to provide her free space; that is, the unfortunate circumstances of her enslavement strongly urged her to seek freedom, during the first period of her poetic maturity, for meaningful movement in her inner, mental world. White folks—especially white males, to be sure—could not have felt such urgency to be free. Kant, for example, could luxuriate with impunity in the world of philosophical speculation. His situation was hardly desperate, and the consequences of indulging his interior space for philosophical contemplation would surely never have resulted in a curbing of his mental activity.

Discovery in her own time that Wheatley was a serious critic of the so-called enlightened age of reason, which ironically still sanctioned slavery, surely would have brought about for her a curbing of her poetic voice, if not a silencing of that voice. That some guessed her potential for criticism is made plain by the Boston crowd's rejection of her February 29, 1772, proposal for a volume. We should also bring forward the reluctance of the Old South Congregational Church to allow her baptism, marking for our poet the failure of several years of attempting to prove herself "worthy." Such degradation of her person did not bring Wheatley the reassurance of public acceptance she doubtlessly wished, hence "forcing" her to seek within a space in which to be free.

As we now understand, Wheatley's "Long Poem," in particular, provides her the room, the space, to realize, at least for a brief time, the joy of freedom. It is "On Imagination," within which she most powerfully articulates her evolving poetics of imagination, that most fully yields to her an absolute space, anticipating a Kantian noumenon. Indeed, this space reifies for her a moment of absolute morality, a "Resistless beauty," as she puts it in "Thoughts," which rejects the enslavement of one's fellow beings.

When, in the very first line of "On Imagination," Wheatley names imagination "imperial queen," she announces to any one conscientious enough to grasp her experiment that she has already promoted imagination to supreme faculty, here resonating with Giordano Bruno's courageous pronouncement. The remainder of the poem establishes just how this poet accomplishes her rebellion; to be sure the medium of this rebellion is her choice of words, wherein those words are arranged in "a beauteous order." This order bespeaks certainly her awareness of the regular rhythm of the heroic couplet, tinctured with recollection of her African linguistic penchant for breath phrasing (see "African

Origins" in the *Liberation* volume). Even so, the order Wheatley actually seeks moves far beyond that of rhythmic lines. Indeed, what she intensely desires, and discovers for a time, is the new order of a world bereft of slavery, a world in which a creative genius, Wheatley, may luxuriate, if only briefly.

Just so, "On Imagination," in its entirety, constitutes a third and comprehensive heterocosm. This third heterocosm, which encompasses the whole poem, comprehends imagination; memory, as in the play on avarice/slavery in the "subject passions"; the subordination of fancy to imagination; and two already identified internal heterocosms. Surely this poem, as a self-conscious construction, gives Wheatley her most ecstatic feeling of the sublime. Surely this poem embodies the essence of romanticism!

In spite of this major accomplishment, which she released to the aesthetic world, in her own time Wheatley appears to have been touted as some sort of public entertainment; Oddell, her principal biographer, tells us that the poet "performed" her so-called occasional poems for guests in the Wheatley mansion, hence finding herself playing the role of entertainer. So when she arrived in London on June 17, 1773, she quickly and predictably became a species of circus act for further on-demand performances. This circumstance of serving as a sort of public exhibition surely, even if ironically, worked in her favor, for this culture ignored the intense seriousness of her internal poetic undertaking. It is significant to consider that, as none of her three-part "Long Poem" had seen print back in Boston (although a version of "On Recollection" was printed in London in March 1772), Wheatley first published her "Long Poem" for the London crowd.

Surely no one there took her poems seriously enough to recognize the extent of her pointed criticism of white folks' celebration of freedom while at the same time refusing to extend their "enlightened" dispositions to embrace the total abolition of slavery. Toward the end of the eighteenth century, nevertheless, philosophic aesthetes, social theorists, and certain poets began to catch up to Wheatley's already registered romantic perception of the imaginative faculty. One with the aesthetic temperament of Samuel Taylor Coleridge, for example, while his own romantic leanings were evolving, could not, if he read her phenomenal "On Imagination," have but been moved by it. As we will shortly see and as I have hinted now for some time, Coleridge did in fact examine salient portions of this poem. His interest in this poem, moreover, evidences a great deal more than simple aesthetic concern.

While I have suggested connections between Wheatley and Coleridge several times, the moment has now arrived to elaborate on those connections and to establish new ones. As we have seen, Wheatley, Kant, and Coleridge all agree that display of the artist's capacity to harness the productive power of imagination manifests an aesthetic indication that that true artist is a genius. A second area of agreement becomes evident as all three promote imagination as a unifier of the mental faculties. As well, Wheatley and Coleridge, but not Kant, raise the imagination to supreme faculty for artists of genius, although we should point out that Coleridge postpones such an unqualified elevation until *Biographia Literaria.*

Another connection to, or bridge between, Wheatley and Coleridge becomes established when we learn that, early in their careers (before and after the publication of *Lyrical Ballads*), Wordsworth and Coleridge shared libraries. It thus becomes tantamount to a certainty that Coleridge would have read Clarkson's *Slavery and Commerce,* containing the hymns to the morning and evening, salient lines from "On Imagination," and the entirety of the letter of attestation as to the authenticity of Wheatley's authorship. It is certainly worth pointing out that, while he does give a sampling of Latin poetry in *Slavery and Commerce,* the lines from Wheatley make up the only English poetry in the volume, suggesting that any English poet reading *Slavery and Commerce* would have been drawn to Wheatley's selections. As such a generous and accurate sampling of Wheatley's poetry implies more than casual acquaintance with the 1773 *Poems,* I posit that Clarkson owned his own copy of *Poems.*

Coleridge's preoccupation with the slavery question, along with the fact that Clarkson was the principal dynamic force—"the moral steam engine," as Coleridge phrased it—behind the British abolition movement argues that Clarkson and Coleridge would have shared the 1773 *Poems.* This sharing, however, could not have taken place until after Coleridge and Wordsworth met the Clarksons for the first time on November 17, 1799. Both Coleridge and Wordsworth, nevertheless, were, as we shall soon observe, already quite familiar with Clarkson's *Slavery and Commerce.*

Still another strong connection between Wheatley and Coleridge becomes evident when we note Coleridge's energetic pact with Robert Southey, made in 1794, to set up a pantisocracy, or utopian society, in America. When Gilbert Imlay's *Topographical Description* came out first in 1792 (later editions in 1793 and 1797), both poets would have been, as a matter of course, much interested in what was surely at the time one of the most thorough geographical descriptions of the recently established United States. From Coleridge's perspective, he would have no doubt found the lines Imlay selected from "On Imagination," those including the first of the two internal heterocosms, to have been most diverting, for reasons we will soon adumbrate.

Coleridge established his preoccupation with the slavery question early in his career when, in June 1792, his "Ode on the Slave-Trade," cast in Greek sapphics, was awarded the Brown Gold Medal while Coleridge was a freshman at Cambridge University. Significantly, on June 16, 1795, Coleridge delivered his first of at least two lectures on slavery (we lack the text of his 1798 homily condemning the slave trade given at Taunton). Titled "Lecture on the Slave-Trade," Coleridge refers to Clarkson's *Slavery and Commerce* twice. So we know he read Clarkson's electrifying text with real interest; as well, it would be absurd to suppose he ignored the Wheatley selections. In Coleridge's "Lecture," he extols the imaginative faculty as "truth-painting Imagination" ("Lecture," 248). That the imagination, the creative faculty, produces painterly manifestations of truth describes much of Wheatley's approach to poetic composition. Had Coleridge already, by this date, looked into Wheatley's *Poems*?

The following year, Coleridge acquired a copy of John Stedman's newly published *Narrative of a Five Years' Expedition against the Revolted Negroes of Surinam*, which quotes the same passage Clarkson had earlier selected from "On Imagination" (but with errors that are not present in Clarkson) and follows that quote with the ecphonesis: "What can be more beautiful and sublime?" (Stedman 363). In a letter to Southey of September 30, 1799, Coleridge quotes from Stedman's *Narrative* a passage that is only twenty pages removed from Stedman's citation of the lines from Wheatley's "On Imagination" (*Collected Letters*, 535).

Pertinent to our discussion of Stedman are Kathleen Coburn's pregnant suggestions that Stedman's text may have prompted Coleridge to mine it for some of the imagery Coleridge used in *Kubla Khan*. In *The Notebooks of Samuel Taylor Coleridge, Volume 1, 1794–1804, Part 2,* edited by Coburn, she points out that Coleridge was especially captivated by Stedman's description of the torture of Africans (vultures consuming carrion on a gallows), material that is also from the Stedman chapter from which Coleridge quoted in his Southey letter. Coburn's fascinating observations strengthen the impact that this chapter containing the lines from Wheatley's "On Imagination" did have on Coleridge's own imagination (*Notebook: Notes,* n. 124). Coleridge assuredly found himself situated in a curiously ideal locus to encounter text(s) by Phillis Wheatley.

In addition, we have noted that Coleridge for a while (before 1817) maintained an intense relationship with the Clarksons as they assisted him in his struggle against opium addiction. Certainly this period would have, perhaps once again, brought Coleridge into close contact with Wheatley's *Poems on Various Subjects, Religious and Moral.* Naming Wheatley's volume also calls to mind the fact that, several years before his addiction problems settled in, on April 16, 1796, Coleridge published his first volume of poetry, titled *Poems on Various Subjects.* Now while this title is hardly unique, given all the other connections to Wheatley we have made, along with the knowledge that Wheatley's *Poems* had been reissued in London in 1786 and again in 1789, it is tempting to claim more than simple coincidence between the titles of these two volumes of poetry.

In general, the other connections between Wheatley and Coleridge may be delineated as those occurring before 1800 and those after 1800. Regarding the period prior to 1800, we still need to assess first an incident approaching plagiarism of a portion of "On Imagination" in an untitled poem Coleridge placed within his newspaper venture of 1796, the *Watchman.* Next we take up the important relationship that developed between Coleridge and Blumenbach while Coleridge was in Germany from September 1798 to July of the following year. From this vantage point, we will be better prepared to evaluate what impact, if any, Wheatley's theoretics of imagination may have exercised on Coleridge's *Biographia Literaria* (dictated in 1815 but not published until 1817).

While not often rehearsed, Coleridge's tendency toward plagiarism has long been known. Jack Stillinger holds that his eventual "drug addiction sapped his strength and will," prompting him to become "reliant on sources that he does not credit" (Abrams and Stillinger, *Norton Anthology* 418). In *Coleridge, The Damaged Archangel,* Norman Fruman tells us that, much earlier (before addiction became a problem), the pressures of trying to put out a multipaged issue of his first newspaper, the *Watchman,* every eight days (to avoid paying the weekly stamp tax), while at the same time incurring the vicissitudes of his recent marriage to Sara Fricker (a baby was on the way), may have contributed to Coleridge's decision to initiate his plagiarism schemes. Fruman, speaking specifically about the *Watchman,* nevertheless insists that "The problem with Coleridge, then as later, is that he deliberately puts forward borrowed material including poetry, as *original*" (Fruman 37; emphasis in original).

One of these so-called original offerings used to fill out an issue of the *Watchman* contains an untitled poem not included in any of Coleridge's *Poetical Works* published in his lifetime, but collected by Ernest Hartley Coleridge in his 1912 *Complete Poetical Works of Samuel Taylor Coleridge,* where it is given the title, "Ver Perpetuum" or "Perpetual Spring." This poem contains several images that are arguably so close to the imagery within the first internal heterocosm, which depicts an eternally possible spring, of "On Imagination" as to indicate not merely similarities but borrowings.

While Clarkson's selection from "On Imagination" included the fancy as subordinate and imagination as agent of great mental force passages, the abolitionist's excerpt does not have the first internal heterocosm. But Imlay's choice from "On Imagination" does. Recall that Imlay had published his *Topographical Description* in 1792 and again in 1793. Wil Verhoeven, Imlay's biographer, states that, motivated by their "utopian emigration scheme," both Southey and Coleridge had "enthusiastically read" Imlay's *Topographical Description,* and Coleridge's biographer of his early years, Richard Holmes, also attests that Coleridge had read Imlay's *Topographical Description.* Unless we are prepared to hold that Coleridge stubbornly avoided Imlay's concentrated examination of Wheatley, we must conclude that Coleridge definitely did read Imlay's choice lines from "On Imagination" ranging from "*Imagination!* who can sing thy force?" through the last line of the first internal heterocosm, "And nectar sparkle on the blooming rose."

While it is certainly relevant to our present discourse that we establish Coleridge's knowledge and reading of Clarkson's and Imlay's selections of salient lines from "On Imagination," we should also bring into our consideration the fact that Coleridge takes much of his material for his *Watchman* number 4 from the earlier "Lecture on the Slave-Trade." We should note, nevertheless, that the "Lecture" includes no poetry. What it does contain, however, are several trenchant observations about imagination. In the opening paragraph of his sermon, delivered April 16, 1795, Coleridge notes that "our proper employment" is "To develop the powers of the Creator," thus aligning himself with such thinkers as Kant (as in a manifestation of the dynamically sublime), Schleiermacher, and of course Wheatley in "On Imagination." "Our

Almighty Parent," so Coleridge continues from above, "hath therefore given to us Imagination that stimulates to the attainment of *real* excellence by the contemplation of splendid Possibilities" ("Lecture" 235; emphasis in original).

Just a few lines below this positive position toward the imaginative faculty, nevertheless, Coleridge, apparently wishing to curb his enthusiasm, remarks, "the evils arising from the formation of imaginary wants" (236). Then, toward the conclusion of the homily, we encounter Coleridge's positing a "truth-painting Imagination" (248). Given the period of these remarks (he and Wordsworth were not yet planning *Lyrical Ballads*), Coleridge's ambiguity toward imagination may be taken as a moment of transition between the old, neoclassical suspicion of imagination, but predicting the coming of a positive revaluation. Even so, once again we must admit that Wheatley had already in 1773 arrived at a characteristically romantic assessment of the power of imagination.

The following year, during which Coleridge brought out the fourth number of his *Watchman,* although his interest in imagination had not diminished, his ambiguity persisted, as he called imagination "a restless faculty" (*Watchman* 4: 131), evoking Charron's guarded position. As in the earlier "Lecture," Coleridge repeats his emphasis on "the powers of the Creator" (132), this emphasis occurring only a few lines before the untitled poem.

Now we are prepared to examine Coleridge's untitled poem from *Watchman* 4 in terms of Wheatley's "Long Poem," as I am convinced that Coleridge's curiosity regarding Wheatley led him to seek out a copy of her *Poems*. Having done so would have inevitably brought him into contact with "On Recollection," "Thoughts on the Works of Providence," and of course the entirety of "On Imagination." When we juxtapose the texts of Coleridge's untitled poem and Wheatley's first internal heterocosm, we immediately detect some striking similarities.

Coleridge's untitled piece is as follows:

> The early Year's fast-flying Vapours stray
> In shadowing Trains across the orb of Day:
> And we, poor Insects of a few short Hours,
>   Deem it a world of Gloom.
> Were it not better hope a nobler doom
> Proud to believe, that with more active powers

> On rapid many-coloured Wing
> We thro' one bright perpetual Spring
> Shall hover round the Fruits and Flowers
> Screen'd by those Clouds & chereish'd by those
>   Showers! (*Watchman*, 132)

Wheatley's first internal heterocosm reads:

> Though *Winter* frowns to *Fancy's* raptur'd eyes
> The fields may flourish, and gay scenes arise;
> The frozen deeps may break their iron bands,
> And bid their waters murmur o'er the sands.
> Fair *Flora* may resume her fragrant reign,
> And with her flow'ry riches deck the plain;
> *Sylvanus* may diffuse his honours round,
> And all the forest may with leaves he crown'd:
> Show'rs may descend, and dews their gems disclose,
> And nectar sparkle on the blooming rose. (66–67)

While both essayist and poet concern themselves with, to quote Coleridge, developing creative powers approaching those of the Deity, "the powers of the Creator" (*Watchman* 4: 132), it is somewhat ironic that Coleridge gets to his notion for developing one's creative powers by way of wishing to possess such powers in order first to express mankind's vicious discontent, which, nevertheless, eventually promises to move mankind, "by new combinations of those powers to imitate his [God's] creativeness." So, according to Coleridge, this sort of awareness promises that "from such enlargement of mind Benevolence will necessarily follow" (132). It would appear, then, that Coleridge would have his audience believe that possession of a poet's disposition toward creativity would soften her or his very soul toward the evil practice of slavery. Good for Coleridge! And surely Wheatley would agree, for the whole of "On Imagination," it appears to me, would have its readers follow just such a path.

Coleridge, here reproducing the generous spirit of the earlier homily, invites his readers to enter a world parallel to Wheatley's first internal heterocosm, one of perpetual spring and significantly absent of the blight of slavery.

Serving as an introduction to Coleridge's untitled poem, this introduction also reproduces the struggle to be free, which Wheatley advances in her fifty-three-line poem. The road toward freedom in Wheatley's heterocosm, with its determination to overcome the frowns of Winter (white folks) must have struck Coleridge as an equally difficult journey, one that he calls "a long and dark Process" (*Watchman* 4: 132).

Now we are prepared to weigh close parallels of vocabulary that obtain between the two tracts quoted above. Coleridge evokes the spring by stating that "The early Year's" heavenly signs of the passage of time "stray / In shadowing Trains" moving "across the orb of Day," bringing us, his readers, into the season of spring. In "Thoughts," Wheatley tells us that the warmth of the sun, Coleridge's "orb of Day," yields "ev'ry flow'ry birth" on the earth which moves "Vast through her orb" (44) or orbit round the sun. Coleridge's "shadowing Trains" resonate nicely with Wheatley's "mental train" in "Thoughts" (48) or her "leader of the mental train" (67) of "On Imagination." To be sure, both poets were very likely familiar with trains of thought in the King James Bible and in Thomas Hobbes's "traynes" of thought in the *Leviathan*.

In Coleridge's poem, the poet takes us from the gloomy prospect of "vices and discontent" to a "nobler" world reachable by means of "more active powers." In "Thoughts," Wheatley closely predicts Coleridge's "more active powers" when she describes the action of the "mental train" which "gives improv'd thine [i.e., her readers'] active pow'rs" (48) as we awake from the world of dream. Coleridge asserts that we attain this state of "more active powers" by the transport of "rapid many-coloured Wing." In "On Imagination," and in the lines excerpted by both Clarkson and Imlay, Wheatley maintains that the "pinions" of imagination "surpass the wind" and thereby provide mental transport to a better world. Her morning hymn, in the passage Clarkson gives us, describes the "Harmonious lays" sung by members of "the feather'd race" who "shake the painted plume." As Coleridge's "many-coloured Wing" presents an unusual image, Coleridge has here, in his "many-coloured Wing," conflated Wheatley's "painted plume" with her wings of transport.

As both poets move directly to their realms of abiding spring, the connection between these two texts strengthens. Whereas Coleridge attests "one bright perpetual Spring," Wheatley, more finite in her construction, draws an arresting contrast between frowning winter (white folks) and flourishing fields, conjured within her "mental optics." In Wheatley's much earlier "perpetual Spring," iron bands become broken and the fair goddess of flowers reigns eternally, her "flow'ry riches" decking the plain of her heterocosm. Coleridge's spring gives us "Showers" we may wish to cherish, yet Wheatley's leaves us with "Show'rs" whose "dews [may] their gems disclose, / And nectar [may] sparkle on the blooming rose" (67), a far more elaborate "painting" of a perdurable spring. We may observe as well that, while both poets depict a world cut off from the horrors of slavery, Wheatley's more highly developed heterocosm (does Coleridge's depiction actually qualify as a heterocosm?) chronicles a fully realized romantic construct. What we may have just witnessed in this episode of intellectual/artistic borrowing illustrates well John Livingston Lowes's description, made in reference to his analysis of the sources for "Kubla Khan," of Coleridge's "preternatural visualizing faculty" (336) for harnessing his incredible memory of practically all he read.

One additional continuum of thought we should register before we leave the present examination concerns Coleridge's "truth painting" phrase in the earlier "Lecture" and his altered phrasing in *Watchman* 4: "now Imagination ought to paint to us" (139). Imlay, perhaps owing something to Wheatley, as I have suggested, early on in his *Topographical Description* traces "as fine a body of land as imagination can paint" (77). In "On Recollection," Wheatley asserts that Phoebe, as "heav'nly *phantom*," "paints the actions done / By ev'ry tribe beneath the rolling sun" (63), and in "Niobe in Distress . . . ," one of her two epyllia, and "To S.M. a Young *African* Painter, on Seeing His Works," Wheatley self-consciously presents two elaborate examples of ekphrasis. Wheatley's association of painting with creative acts of the mind strikes me as the kind of aesthetic theorizing (about how a poet may create a text) that would have captured the attention of Coleridge as he was making himself into a poet, and a romantic poet at that.

When we add the preceding remarks to all the other evidence we have accumulated, the notion that certain of Wheatley's texts could have served a constructive role in the evolution of Coleridge's aesthetics impresses me as, at the very least, an indication that a close intellectual and transatlantic conversation between these two poets has indeed taken place. The fact is, moreover, we have only delineated the availability of Wheatley's texts to Coleridge to its midpoint. That is, we are about to find that what we have viewed at this juncture provides us with roughly half the evidence accruing to the literary relationship obtaining between these two poet-thinkers.

The next episode embracing Coleridge's very likely familiarity with Wheatley's texts, comprehending all poems by her in the 1773 *Poems,* takes us to the Continent, specifically into the circle of Johann F. Blumenbach, father of physical anthropology and legendary lecturer and conversationalist. Initially embarking for Germany with Wordsworth and his sister Dorothy on September 18, 1798, Coleridge eventually located in Blumenbach's Göttingen. In *Coleridge: Early Visions,* the only biography I have found that traces in detail Coleridge's German adventure, Richard Holmes declares that the "lectures of Blumenbach . . . drew him like a magnet" (196). Especially appealing to Coleridge, Holmes notes, were "Blumenbach's investigations into natural history," doubtlessly taking Coleridge toward examination of Blumenbach's *On the Natural Variety of Mankind,* which had interested Kant, and his *Contributions to Natural History,* wherein the anthropologist praises the poems of Phillis Wheatley.

In a letter to Humphry Davy (important scientist, occasional poet [he assisted Wordsworth with his revision of *Lyrical Ballads*] and, by the late 1820s, no longer intimate with Coleridge and, unhappily, a promoter of racial genetics allegedly designed to eliminate Africans and Native Americans) of June 7, 1800, Coleridge states, "I think of translating Blumenbach's manual of natural History" (*Letters,* 590; the editor, Earl L. Griggs, footnotes this history as Blumenbach's *Beyträge zur Naturgeschichte,* the 1790 *Contributions to Natural History*). Although Coleridge does not accomplish this task of rendering Blumenbach's German into English, his plan to pursue its translation attests Coleridge's substantial interest in this text; more to the point, his preoccupation with this German text establishes, irrefutably, Coleridge's knowledge regarding the name and reputation of Phillis Wheatley.

Coleridge's positive and productive months spent with Blumenbach (despite the death in April 1799 of his son Berkeley) may be measured by his cultivation of Blumenbach's son and by "the tremendous party" given for the maturing British poet "by Professor Blumenbach" upon his departure from Göttingen on June 24, 1799. When Coleridge returned to Britain in the following month, he brought with him not merely a plan to translate Blumenbach's *Contributions* but also the memory of conversations about abolition, a subject that clearly concerned both poet and anthropologist. This inevitable subject would surely have involved Blumenbach's producing his evidentiary copy of Wheatley's *Poems,* of which he was a champion, hence inviting Coleridge's opinion regarding them.

Still another appreciation Coleridge carried with him from his German days was a deep and abiding determination to acquire comprehension of the philosophy of Kant, especially of his *Critique of Judgment.* Coleridge's keen interest in Kant becomes evident in *Biographia Literaria, or Biographical Sketches of My Literary Life and Opinions,* particularly in his preoccupation with the problem of creative genius. Coleridge's attempts in his literary/intellectual autobiography to grasp and apply Kant's theoretics regarding creative genius appear most vividly in his analysis of the imaginative faculty. Once again, perhaps unexpectedly, we will discover that the work of Phillis Wheatley, especially her "Long Poem," interfaces in fecund ways with Coleridge's theoretics of imagination.

Parallels between these two poets surface early on in *Biographia,* as when Coleridge describes his Latin grammar school reading of Shakespeare. As early as 1767, as we have established, Wheatley has given us concrete evidence that she had absorbed the great bard's texts well enough to incorporate into her "To the University of Cambridge in New-England" a passage from *Julius Caesar;* this poem was one of her earliest poetic efforts. Wheatley was, moreover, at this early date, heavily engaged in Latin studies. Coleridge carefully points out that his schoolmaster taught him that, among "the truly great poets" like Shakespeare, Milton, Homer, and Vergil, "there is a reason assignable not only for every word, but for the position of every word" (*Biographia* 1: 9). Herein resides the origins for Coleridge's later organicism.

For our purposes, nonetheless, we quickly recognize that both Wheatley and Coleridge received remarkably similar schooling. To be sure, Coleridge went on to enjoy the better part of a university education at Cambridge, England, only occasionally venturing into the making of verse. Wheatley, with no prospect of acquiring a formal university education, began writing verses, certainly by 1765 when only about twelve, and very probably at that time she began to manifest an urgency to compose; Wheatley opens the 1767 "To . . . Cambridge" with the arresting assertion that "an intrinsic ardor prompts [me] to write." Already the need to compose comes, by her own testimony, from the soul of a poet.

In addition to the close connections describing their respective early educations, Coleridge makes an observation, also in Chapter I, about dreams, "by which the blind fancy would fain interpret to the mind the painful sensations of distempered sleep" (*Biographia* 1: 11). As we have noted, in "On Recollection" and "Thoughts," Wheatley expresses a similar concern for the effect of dreams. "On Recollection" summons up "the long-forgotten ... from night," which allows the poet to paint "the actions done / By ev'ry tribe beneath the rolling sun" (62–63), enabling her to recall the horrific Middle Passage. "Thoughts" conjures from sleep both a realm of absolute freedom, wherein "ideas range / Licentious and unbounded," as well as the memories of "vengeance" and the "lab'ring passions [which] struggle for a vent" (47).

It is in this same chapter 1 wherein Coleridge introduces his intermittent preoccupation with the subject of genius. According to Coleridge, "it is peculiar to original genius to become less and less *striking* in proportion to its success in improving the taste and judgment" (*Biographia* 1: 24). Here Coleridge interestingly and perhaps subliminally adopts early on the language (in his use of the words "genius," "taste," and "judgment") of Kant from the *Critique of Judgment,* especially that of his "Dialectic of the Aesthetical Judgment." Coleridge's concerted interest in genius intensifies as he approaches his famous chapter 13, an analysis of the artist/poet's imagination. So we should not be surprised to learn that the action of the poet's imagination comes to serve as touchstone in Coleridge for genius. What is certainly surprising, nonetheless, is to discover that later the language Coleridge applies while traveling toward his well-known analysis precisely parallels, at almost every step, that used by Phillis Wheatley.

Clearly when Coleridge introduces the concept of imagination as the "esemplastic" power or the power to *coadunate* (from the Latin meaning "to make one with"), he attests the proximity to his major philosophical and aesthetic breakthrough in his analysis of the creative imagination, which shortly follows in the famous explication of chapter 13 (see *Biographia* 1: 168–69 and 168n–70n). In a finely researched three-page footnote to the notion of shaping into one, James Engell presents an ostensibly convincing listing of German sources for Coleridge's understanding. While he names possible sources among the works of Kant and Friedrich Schelling (his major work, *The System of Transcendental Idealism,* which would unite philosophical transcendentalism and a philosophy of nature, had appeared in 1800), Engell omits any mention of Phillis Wheatley.

Engell insists that the operative German word that predicts the unifying effect of a creative imagination is *Einbildungskraft,* the expression employed by Kant and later by Schelling. Recall that already in 1773, Wheatley joined imagination and force in the important line, "*Imagination!* who can sing thy force[?]." In the same lengthy footnote, Engell also states that "the notion that the imagination forms [a unity] as it blends and actively coalesces associations and perceptions was quite common by the 1790s" among German aestheticians (*Biographia,* 1: 169n). And it is, moreover, such writers as Kant and Schelling who "add the notion of a dialectic synthesis of opposition into one unity." By the 1790s, nevertheless, Wheatley had already arrived at this grasp, practically a generation earlier. Certainly it is true that Coleridge names Schelling (and Kant, of course) as major influences on shaping his theoretics of creative imagination.

I am herein arguing that pertinent lines expressing Wheatley's own peculiar analysis of the imaginative faculty were available, not only to Coleridge, but even to others of the German males concerned with analysis of the creative imagination. Considering the times, women were not particularly celebrated as independent thinkers (a deliberate understatement). So when Engell opens his chapter in *The Creative Imagination,* which is devoted to Coleridge, with this sweeping observation, "In forming his concept of the imagination, Coleridge draws on nearly every other [he might as well have said 'male'] writer who discusses the subject" (328), we should not be surprised, regrettably even in 1981, by Engell's omission of even a mention of Phillis Wheatley. After all, she is only a woman, an American, and an African American at that.

Despite all the negatives militating against taking the work of Wheatley seriously, then as now, Coleridge gives strong indications that he did take Wheatley quite seriously. In his famous chapter 13, for example, he declares that fancy deals exclusively with fixities and definites. "The Fancy is indeed," Coleridge continues, "no other than a mode of Memory emancipated from the order of time and space; and blended with and modified by that empirical phenomenon of the will, which we express by the word CHOICE" (*Biographia,* 305). Is this operation of the mind not identical with Wheatley's "Now here, now there, the roving *Fancy* flies / Till some lov'd object strikes her wand'ring eyes, / Whose silken fetters all the senses bind, / And soft captivity involves the mind" (65)? To Wheatley, according to these lines, the fancy flies here and there, "emancipated by the order of time and space," as the will of the poet's mind luxuriates amid its freedom of movement, led by a desire (will) to satisfy the mind which is only brought to focus by "some lov'd object." Just so, has Wheatley, in her description of fancy, not predicted Coleridge's "CHOICE"?

As such, fancy is not in and of itself a power of re-creativity. Rather fancy remains a faculty that serves as "drapery," Coleridge's consistent assignment in *Biographia* for fancy (as on 1: 24 and 2: 18). In another passage in the second volume of *Biographia,* Coleridge describes "fanciful circumstances," that is, the images bespeaking "the animal impulse" Coleridge detects in Shakespeare's *Venus and Adonis,* "which form its dresses and its scenery" (*Biographia,* 2: 22). In "On Imagination," as she brings her experiment to a close, recording the power of her or the poet's imagination to paint alternative worlds, Wheatley affectively relates that "I reluctant leave the pleasing views, / Which *Fancy* dresses to delight the Muse" (68; "Muse" on this occasion refers to the poet).

One need not press these instances of parallel grasp of how fancy functions in the poetic process to determine that, if actual borrowing has not taken place, at the very least, we encounter in Coleridge's descriptions of "fancy" a case of what John Livingston Lowes has termed "that prehensile associative faculty" which is Coleridge's. It is, nevertheless, when we investigate their respective understandings of the creative imagination that we witness two brilliant minds conducting an integrative, transatlantic conversation. Wheatley's imagination constitutes a great force of mind that can bring the poet to new knowledge of "the thund'ring God" (66), as we discover later in Kant's descriptions of the feeling of the dynamic sublime, approximating ecstasy. As Wheatley puts it, anticipating Kant's stirring depictions, the power, the force, of imagination enables the poet and her readers to "grasp the mighty whole ... in one view" (66).

By the time of his chapter 13 in *Biographia,* Coleridge, who has throughout his career registered case after case detailing the human determination to imitate the Divine power to create, settles on the creative power of the imagination to accomplish best his objective, which is finally to construe a suitable delineation of such a desideratum. Wheatley, of course, long before had arrived at such an understanding of the creative imagination to replicate the Divine power, this articulation occurring when the poet was only nineteen years of age. While Wheatley in her "Long Poem" clearly casts her grasp of how the imagination functions as the poet's reason, and as we have seen here predicting Wordsworth, Coleridge attempts to distinguish imagination, at one level as the province of all persons but at another, higher level as a power of creativity available only to artists of genius. What causes this power of creativity subsequently to be recognizable as attendant upon all minds of genius is its power to unify.

As we have seen earlier, Kant concerns himself with a similar problem wherein he theorizes that the imagination, in addition to serving as mediator between the senses and the understanding, also displays a unifying capacity. In Coleridge, this capacity to unify resides in the second level of imagination. The first level or the primary imagination holds "the living Power and prime Agent of all human Perception," which functions "as a repetition in the finite mind of the eternal act of creation in the infinite I AM" (*Biographia* 1: 304). Here Coleridge essentially describes the ordinary human's ability to perceive the idea of the Divine. The higher level of imagination, what Coleridge calls "the secondary imagination," Coleridge conceives to be "an echo" of the primary; that is, as I see it, this level is secondary insofar as it extends, by virtue of its location in a mind of artistic genius, the primary imagination.

When the operation of the secondary imagination accelerates its creative capacity, becoming itself creative, then, no longer a mere echo, it "dissolves, diffuses, dissipates in order to re-create" (*Biographia* 1: 304). Interestingly enough, Wheatley speaks in "Thoughts" of how God's works become "diffus'd abroad" (47) or in "On Recollection" of how fair Phoebe's power moves in sleep through "the unbounded regions of the mind, / Diffusing light celestial and refin'd" (62), while in one of her elegies death becomes empowered to "dissolve the sky" (51). As well, Coleridge maintains that the secondary imagination, as a living power, "struggles to idealize and to unify" (*Biographia* 1: 304). When Wheatley insists that "all thy works"—that is, the products of her creative imagination—"are wrought" "In full perfection" (67), has she not by application of "the leader of the mental train," her imagination, transformed her poem into an idealized unity?

Concluding Remarks: Is Wheatley the Progenetrix of Romanticism?

Among the many male authors Coleridge cites numbers Giordano Bruno, with whose martyrdom this monograph opened. Coleridge is impressed enough by Bruno, perhaps as much by his martyrdom as by what he has to say in celebration of imagination, to speak of him in *Biographia* several times. As for mention of Phillis Wheatley, we search in vain. Glaringly, Coleridge does not shrink from failing to name two other women whose work he "borrowed," the Danish poet Frederica Brun and Mary ("Perdita") Robinson, whom Coleridge knew and admired (see Fruman 27–29, 45). Indeed, it appears that the patriarchy of the era would not permit the naming of creative women. In its infinite wisdom, such a phenomenon as an original, thinking woman was, quite simply, an impossibility. This same reductive thinking has, of course, mitigated toward preventing proper recognition of our subject.

In an Oxford Reader on *Aesthetics,* Linda Nochlin, a specialist on feminist art history, insists in "Women, Art, and Power," that, particularly during the era of the late eighteenth and early nineteenth centuries, a woman was considered to be "an object rather than a creator of art." At that time, it was thought—by the patriarchy, of course—that it was patently ridiculous for a woman "to insert herself actively into the realm of history by means of work or engagement in political struggle" (72). Even so, Phillis Wheatley, having searched for and found her own agency as a poet (see Shields, *Phillis Wheatley's Poetics of Liberation* passim), empowered herself by going so far as attempting to create herself an independent professional, with publication of her 1773 *Poems*. At the same time, Wheatley did in fact insert herself as a political figure in the American quest for freedom for everyone, regardless of race.

We find Wheatley time after time enacting each of the tenets Iain McCalman asserts, in his "Introduction" to the cornucopia of information,

An Oxford Companion to the Romantic Age: British Culture, 1776–1832, which he serves as general editor, that "British romanticism ... was nourished by ... a transcendent ideal that elevated creative imagination, individual genius, and the inward self over the prosaic requirements of scribbling for a living" (2). Surely by this juncture we need not rehearse Wheatley's elevation of imagination, her intellectual individualism ascertaining her genius, or her palpable turn inward to express her personal quest for the moments of freedom she boldly grants herself. We must quickly reiterate, nevertheless, that Wheatley arrives at these self-discoveries before 1776 (recall McCalman's *1776–1832*) and that she does soon the opposite side of the Pond.

Interestingly enough, McCalman and his many contributors, while they do spend time with Kant and Schelling, give no space to Wheatley or, for that matter, to Bruno. As well, these same contributors speak on several occasions about the importance to British romanticism of Thomas Clarkson, Gilbert Imlay, and John Stedman, men who all assign at least some space to Phillis Wheatley! As we have observed repeatedly, Wheatley's texts were in fairly broad circulation. Other male authors who exposed themselves to her texts include Voltaire, Blumenbach, Wordsworth, Coleridge, and Grégoire, all of whom were probably joined by Kant, Stewart, and possibly Schleiermacher and Schelling. My point is simply to acknowledge that members of the patriarchy did in fact pay attention to texts by Phillis Wheatley, many of whom actually extolled the value of her texts, perhaps as evidence against targeting Africans for enslavement; but even so we find her again and again to be the subject of much attention. Such a staunch racist as Thomas Jefferson, for example, found himself forced to deal with her texts, if only to denigrate them and then to deny their authenticity.

In the latest (ninth) edition of *A Glossary of Literary Terms,* Meyer H. Abrams and Geoffrey G. Harpham assert that "Representative Romantic works are in fact poems of feelingful meditation which, although often stimulated by a natural phenomenon, are concerned with central human experience and problems" (214). Wheatley's connections to the praxis of *meditatio* ("feelingful meditation") have been enumerated, and her emphasis on the sun as perhaps the most immediately powerful suggestion of an even more powerful Creator is amply evident in her "Thoughts on the Works of Providence," wherein the poet yearns for realization of the promise of freedom for all.

Abrams and Harpham are careful to add that "Many writers," among the romantics, "viewed a human being as endowed with limitless aspiration toward an infinite good envisioned by the faculty of imagination" (214). In our treatment of Wheatley and Coleridge, we have remarked on their mutual preoccupations with the abolishment of slavery (surely an "infinite good"), a concern that each develops in close conjunction with their theoretics of imagination.

William Harmon and Hugh Holman claim, in their most recent edition of *A Handbook to Literature* (the tenth), that "The term," romanticism, "is used in many senses, a recent favorite being that which sees in the romantic mood a psychological desire to escape from unpleasant realities" (456). Surely Wheatley's line describing a world "Oppress'd with woes, a painful endless train" (152) points toward this sentiment, just as her creation of her heterocosms provides an escape. Harmon and Holman expand their explanation of the term to include the characteristics of a "love of nature," "individualism," an "unrestrained imagination," "an interest in human rights," and the application of "the reflective lyric" (456–57)—all issues Wheatley takes up. While Wheatley does not precisely subscribe to what we can think of as a totally unrestrained imagination, she certainly does endorse the power, the force, of imagination when she elevates this re-creative productive faculty to "leader of the mental train."

In the prestigious *Norton Anthology of English Literature: The Romantic Period,* M. H. Abrams and Jack Stillinger sharpen our understanding of romanticism when they underscore the emphasis Harman and Holman place on the meditative lyric by insisting that among romantics, "the 'I'" of lyrics "often is not a conventionally typical lyric speaker, such as the Petrachan lover or Cavalier gallant of Elizabethan and seventeenth-century love poems, but has recognizable traits of the poet's own person and circumstances" (7). Wheatley's readers find themselves exposed to a personalized, identifiable persona who clearly manifests the voice of the poet herself, and not merely in her "Long Poem." Throughout her oeuvre, her poems employ the voice of an "I" that ever registers an individually involved response to persons and events of her time, in addition to her intense interiorization, during the first period of her maturity, of her struggle to be free.

In an effort to correct the patriarchal de-emphasis of prior attitudes toward women, Stillinger and Abrams point out that, while Wordsworth and

Coleridge were developing young poets, "Some of the best regarded poets of the time were women—Anna Barbauld, Charlotte Smith, Mary Robinson—and," so they continue, "Wordsworth and Coleridge (both of whom were junior colleagues of Robinson when she was poetry editor of the *Morning Post* in the late 1790s) looked up to them and learned some of their craft from them" (1). Perhaps it is too much to expect, even at this juncture, that we begin to recognize that all these poets named, men and women, found instruction for their craft from certain of Wheatley's widely available texts.

Another qualifier of the romantic temperament Stillinger and Abrams are careful to take up is the fact that so many of the romantics employ the construction of poetry as a means for an individual poet to pursue her or his idea of the Deity. Pointing out Coleridge's early treatment of his religious consciousness amid his aesthetic explorations, as we noted in the preceding chapter, these editors declare that "Mind, wrote Coleridge in 1801, is 'not passive,' but 'made in God's Image, and that too in the most sublime sense—the Image of the Creator'" (13). I am struck here by how closely these quoted remarks made by Coleridge predict his chapter 13 in *Biographia Literaria*. Stillinger and Abrams, moreover, claim that "Many Romantic writers also agreed that the mind has access beyond sense to the transcendent and the infinite, through a special faculty they called either Reason or Imagination" (13). I should like to modify this claim just a bit to accommodate both Wheatley and Coleridge. Indeed, each of these poets identifies the imagination as that power of mind which enables the poet's connection to the Divine; recall that Wordsworth called this mental power, imagination, the "poet's reason."

Surely by now there can be little lingering doubt that Phillis Wheatley was ably prepared to engage that discourse which was shaping the movement of thought we now refer to as romanticism. What the evidence ascertains is that in fact Wheatley was already expressing the central qualities of romanticism, as proposed by the authorities I have cited throughout this monograph, long before the traditionally recognized lions of the movement. To identify her as a pioneer impresses me as hardly adequate.

Most particularly, we have in this monograph recovered the fact that this considerably sophisticated intellectual anticipated with remarkable acuity the principal tenets of what we have come to call romanticism. After a failure, lasting some 230 years, to recognize this major and now become undeniable achievement, we must pay her the honor she has earned. Henry Louis Gates Jr., one of the nation's most outstanding scholars, has judiciously said that

> The peculiar history of Wheatley's reception by critics has, ironically enough, largely determined the theory of the criticism of the creative writings of Afro-Americans from the eighteenth century to the present time. (79)

So her importance to the study of African American "creative writings" has become irrefutably established. But what about her contributions to other characteristics of culture?

Her contributions to the culture of American women in general have, for example, been underappreciated. In the recent best-selling *Founding Mothers: The Women Who Raised Our Nation,* Cokie Roberts, in a long chapter celebrating Mercy Otis Warren, a poet, dramatist, and historian of the Revolutionary War era, interjects a page and a few lines regarding Wheatley, but no more. Here Wheatley may be viewed as through a crack in the door through which she may be glimpsed, though she is clearly not granted the status of a woman who played the role of a founding mother. I am left wondering, why not?

In the late eighteenth and early nineteenth centuries on the other side of the Pond, that is, in England and the Continent, she did, nevertheless, serve for a time a role that contributed substantially to the flow of thought which yields what we prefer today to identify as romanticism. What I am trying to suggest constitutes a dramatic episode of transatlantic aesthetic conversation, although the direction obviously travels from America to the other side of the Atlantic. Now I fully realize that, certainly for a moment, the flow of thought here looks all wrong. Most of my colleagues may find this direction somewhat disconcerting, for conventional wisdom would have it that—say, until the work of Edgar Allan Poe—significant innovations in literary culture could only have traveled from Europe to America. Yet the upshot of a large part of my scholarship has taught me that America was a fertile ground for new aesthetic/literary experiments, not the least of which was the phenomenon we know to be Phillis Wheatley.

But, but, some may stammer, she is after all only a woman, for that matter only an African, only a slave, and, potentially, most damning of all, only an American. Unlike Coleridge, who penned a lengthy literary autobiography in which he omits acknowledgment of readings that impacted the evolution of his literary aesthetics, particularly the poetry of Phillis Wheatley, let us be honest as we try to set the record straight and give Wheatley her just recognition.

In reference to the Conclusion's subtitle, well, isn't she?

Postscript

What Remains to Be Done

I should like to state that this text merely opens the door to possibilities regarding Wheatley studies abroad; as well, this monograph signals the need for new approaches to Early American Studies in general. For example, someone with great energy and a highly motivated appreciation for literary detection needs to explore how Wheatley was viewed within discourse communities. In England, we have already noted that Frances Reynolds, sister of Sir Joshua Reynolds (artist and aesthete), wrote to Elizabeth Robinson Montagu a letter of September 10, 1794, regarding Phillis Wheatley. Who else in this circle was reading or curious about Wheatley, and what were the possible consequences of such interest? As the Reynolds-Monagu correspondence is still in manuscript (brought to my attention by an excellent young scholar, Zachary Petrea), this kind of investigation requires visiting manuscript repositories, such as those in the British Museum or the Bodleian Library.

I am also left wondering how other women, say on the Continent, were reading Wheatley. It is tempting as well to raise the question of how much more detail close, archival investigation may recover within Continental borders. I daresay the Wordsworth connection bears further examination. Who also read Clarkson, both in England and on the Continent, and may have been prompted to ferret out Wheatley's texts? We are now well prepared to declare that Wheatley's texts were not exclusively sought out as instruments in some socio-anthropological argument for or against slavery, but were enjoyed, during the late eighteenth and early nineteenth centuries, as legitimate aesthetic objects.

Who on the Continent and in Great Britain owned copies of Wheatley's *Poems*, besides Clarkson and Blumenbach? What consequences may be traced regarding such ownership? In addition to ascertaining the fact that Wheatley was an internationally known and touted author, preceding the recognition of Washington Irving by a generation, who is usually accorded the distinction of America's first internationally known author, how does acknowledgment of the substantial role Wheatley played in helping to shape the thought that evolved into romanticism cause literary scholars to reevaluate the long-held notion that America produced no original authors before Irving, James Fenimore Cooper, or Edgar Allan Poe?

This last consideration leads us directly to expose yet another stubbornly held manifestation of conventional wisdom—the seldom investigated but now undeniable proof that substantial and original literary sophistication did in fact exist amid the allegedly ill-prepared population of Colonial and early Revolutionary-era creative artists. What I have in mind are the aesthetic and theoretical accomplishments of such American poets as Mather Byles and Samuel Cooper, whom we have met, but also other literary artists like Thomas Odiorne, whose 1792 *Progress of Refinement* displays a remarkable and arresting understanding of all five of the eighteenth century's aesthetic categories—the sublime, the beautiful, the imagination, taste, and the picturesque.

Disappointingly the recently published *Oxford Handbook of Early American Literature*, edited by Kevin J. Hayes, gives little if any attention even to the possibility of aesthetic sophistication within Colonial and early republican literatures. I am particularly displeased to report this huge text (about 650 pages) makes scant mention of Phillis Wheatley, America's first internationally known author. My efforts throughout my career have largely been devoted to directing attention toward the importance of Phillis Wheatley, certainly a formidable poet. I must, alas, concede failure in this pursuit, at least for the present. I am emboldened to admonish, nevertheless, that I am tenacious of purpose and indefatigable of energy.

One additional undertaking that deserves articulation—I am certain other Wheatley readers will offer additional suggestions—accrues to the fact that many African American women of the nineteenth century took Phillis Wheatley most seriously, both as an inspiration to compose their own poetry and as a source of pride. Such poets as Ann Plato and Frances Watkins Harper, for example, refer to her in their poems. So where is the book on *Phillis Wheatley and African American Women Authors of the Nineteenth Century?* As I am *not* planning such a project, this one is up for grabs.

Chronology

1600	February 17, Giordano Bruno burned at the stake by the Inquisition
1601	Pierre Charron publishes *De la sagesse* (*Of Wisdom*)
1650	Thomas Hobbes publishes *Leviathan*
1708	Shaftesbury's *Characteristics of Men, Manners, Opinions, Times*
1712	Addison's "Pleasures of the Imagination" published in the *Spectator*
1744	Mather Byles's *Poems on Several Occasions*
1753	Phillis Wheatley born in Gambia
1757	Burke's *Philosophical Enquiry into the Origin of Our Ideas of the Sublime and Beautiful*
1760	Joseph Seccombe dies
1761	*Pietas et Gratulatio,* containing two poems by Samuel Cooper
	July 11, Phillis Wheatley sold on the block and named for the slaver, *The Phillis,* which brought her
1762	Lord Kames's *Elements of Criticism*
1765	Wheatley's nonextant letter to Samson Occom, a Mohegan minister, her first known writing
1767	December 21, Wheatley's first published writing, the poem "On Messrs. Hussey and Coffin"
1770	William Billings's *New England Psalm-Singer*
	October 2, "On the Death of the Rev. George Whitefield," published in America but soon after in London, bringing to England announcement of this rara avis and marking Wheatley an international author
1773	May 8, Wheatley embarks on her London adventure but returns to Boston July 26, having been much celebrated
	August 6, Wheatley's *Poems on Various Subjects, Religious and Moral*
	October 18, letter to David Wooster (later a general in the American Revolution) announcing Wheatley's manumission
1784	December 5, Wheatley dies, largely forgotten in the chaos of the American Revolution

1786	Wheatley's reputation revived in Thomas Clarkson's *An Essay on the Slavery and Commerce of the Human Species, Particularly the African*
	Wheatley's *Poems on Various Subjects, Religious and Moral* reprinted in London
1787	Wheatley's *Poems on Various Subjects, Religious and Moral* reprinted in London
1789	Wheatley's *Poems on Various Subjects, Religious and Moral* reprinted in London
1790	Kant's *Critique of Judgment* published early in the year
	Johann F. Blumenbach publishes first edition of his *Contributions to Natural History*, in which he mentions both Wheatley and Clarkson
1792	First edition of Gilbert Imlay's *Topographical Description of the North American Continent* (Second in 1793 and third in 1797)
1796	Coleridge publishes his *Watchman* series; borrows from Wheatley in untitled poem from *Watchman IV* for March 25
1798	Coleridge embarks (with Dorothy and William Wordsworth) for Germany on September 18 but soon locates at Göttingen with Blumenbach
1799	Coleridge leaves Göttingen on June 24; returns to Britain the following month
	During October and November, Coleridge and Wordsworth take their first Lake District tour; they meet the Clarksons on November 17, stay for dinner and spend the night
1800	Coleridge superintends publication of *Lyrical Ballads* (second edition with Wordsworth's long, revised "Preface")
1813	Wheatley's *Poems on Various Subjects, Religious and Moral* appended to an edition of Olaudah Equiano's *Interesting Narrative;* printed in Halifax, England
1815	Parts of Coleridge's *Biographia Literaria* dictated
1816	Wheatley's *Poems on Various Subjects, Religious and Moral* reprinted in London
1817	Coleridge publishes *Biographia Literaria,* in which, several times, he refers, always positively, to Giordano Bruno

Works Cited and Consulted

Abrams, M. H., and Geoffrey Galt Harpham. *A Glossary of Literary Terms*. 9th ed. Boston: Thomas Wadsworth, 2009.

———. *The Mirror and the Lamp: Romantic Theory and the Critical Tradition*. New York: Norton, 1953.

———. *Natural Supernaturalism: Tradition and Revolution in Romantic Literature*. New York: W. W. Norton, 1971.

———, and Jack Stillinger, eds. *The Norton Anthology of English Literature: The Romantic Period*. 7th ed. New York: Norton, 2000.

Adanson, Michel. *A Voyage to Senegal, the Isle of Goree, and the River Gambia*. London: Sir Richard Phillips, 1759.

Addison, Joseph. *The Spectator*. Ed. Donald F. Bond. 4 vols. London: Oxford UP, 1965.

Akenside, Mark. *The Poetical Works of Mark Akenside*. London: George Bell, 1894.

Akers, Charles W. *The Divine Politician: Samuel Cooper and the American Revolution in Boston*. Boston: Northeastern UP, 1982.

———. "'Our Modern Egyptians': Phillis Wheatley and the Whig Campaign against Slavery in Revolutionary Boston." *Journal of Negro History* 60.3 (1975): 397–410.

Allen, William G. *Wheatley, Banneker and Horton*. Boston: Press of Daniel Losing Jr., 1849.

Andrews, William L., Frances Smith Forster, and Trudier Harris, eds. *The Oxford Companion to African American Literature*. New York, Oxford UP, 1997.

Applegate, Ann. "Phillis Wheatley: Her Critics and Her Contribution." *Negro American Literature Forum* 9.4 (1975): 123–26.

Aristotle. *The Complete Works of Aristotle*. Ed. Jonathan Barnes. 2 vols. Princeton, NJ: Princeton UP, 1984.

Augustine. *On the Holy Trinity; Doctrinal Treatises; Moral Treatises*. In Vol. 3 of *Nicene and Post-Nicene Fathers*. Ed. Philip Schaff. Peabody, MA: Hendrickson, 1994.

Bacon, Francis. "Advancement of Learning." In *Critical Essays of the Seventeenth Century*. Ed. J. E. Spingarn. Vol. 1. 1908. Honolulu: UP of the Pacific, 2005. 1–9.

Baker, Houston A., Jr. *The Journey Back: Issues in Black Literature and Culture*. Chicago: U of Chicago P, 1980.

———. *Workings of the Spirit: The Poetics of Afro-American Women's Writing*. Chicago: U of Chicago P, 1991.

Baldwin, James. "Religious Elements in Black Literature." Knoxville: Committee on U of Tennessee Cultural Attractions, 1978.

Balkun, Mary McAleer. "Phillis Wheatley's Construction of Otherness and the Rhetoric of Performed Ideology." *African American Review* 36.1 (Spring 2002): 121–36.

Bassard, Katherine C. *Spiritual Interrogations: Culture, Gender, and Community in Early African American Women's Writing*. Princeton, NJ: Princeton UP, 1999.

Bate, Walter Jackson. *From Classic to Romantic: Premises of Taste in Eighteenth-Century England*. Cambridge, MA: Harvard UP, 1946.

Bayly, Anselm. *The Alliance of Musick, Poetry, and Oratory*. 1978. New York: Garland, 1972.

Baym, Max I. *A History of Literary Aesthetics in America*. New York: Frederick Ungar, 1973.

Berman, Eleanor Davidson. *Thomas Jefferson among the Arts: An Essay in Early American Esthetics*. New York: Philosophical Library, 1947. Baltimore: Penguin, 1971.

Biblia Sacra Latina—the Latin Vulgata. London: Samuel Bagsler & Sons, 1997.

Billings, William. *The New England Psalm Singer* (1770). Ed. Karl Kroeger. Vol. 1 of *The Complete Works of William Billings*. Boston: American Musicological Society and Colonial Society of Massachusetts, 1981.

Blackwell, Albert L. *Schleiermacher's Early Philosophy of Life: Determinism, Freedom, and Phantasy*. Chico, CA: Scholars Press, 1982.

Blumenbach, Johann F. *The Anthropological Treatises of Johann Friedrich Blumenbach*. Trans. Thomas Bendyshe. London: Longman, Green, Longman, Roberts and Green, 1865.

Bolgar, R. R. *The Classical Heritage and Its Beneficiaries*. London: Cambridge UP, 1954.

Bond, Donald F. "'Distrust' of Imagination in English Neo-Classicism." *Philological Quarterly* 14.4 (1935): 54–69.

———. "The Neo-Classical Psychology of the Imagination." *Journal of English Literary History* 4.4 (1937): 245–64.

Boulton, Alexander O. "The American Paradox: Jeffersonian Equality and Racial Science." *American Quarterly* 47.3 (September 1995): 467–93.

Bowie, Andrew. *Aesthetics and Subjectivity: from Kant to Nietzsche.* Manchester: Manchester UP, 1990.

Brown, Gillian. *The Consent of the Governed: The Lockean Legacy in Early American Culture.* Cambridge, MA: Harvard UP, 2001.

Brown, Hallie Quinn. *Homespun Heroines and Other Women of Distinction.* New York: Oxford UP, 1988.

Brown, John. *A Dissertation on the Rise, Union, and Power, the Progression, Separations, and Corruptions of Poetry and Music.* 1763. New York: Garland Publishing, 1971.

Brown, Marshall. *Preromanticism.* Stanford, CA: Stanford UP, 1991.

Burke, Edmund. *Philosophical Enquiry into the Origin of Our Ideas of the Sublime and Beautiful.* Ed. J. T. Boulton. New York: Columbia UP, 1958.

Burnet, Thomas. *The Sacred Theory of the Earth.* London, 1690–91. Carbondale: Southern Illinois UP, 1965.

Byles, Mather. "Bombastic and Grubstreet Style." *The Puritans.* Rev. ed. Perry Miller and Thomas H. Johnson, eds. Vol. 2. New York: Harper and Row, 1963.

———. *God Glorious in the Scenes of the Winter.* Boston: Green for Gookin, 1744.

———. *Poems on Several Occasions.* Boston, 1744.

———. *Poems on Several Occasions.* Introduction by C. Lennart Carlson. New York: Columbia UP, 1942.

Carroll, Frances Laverne, and Mary Meacham. *The Library at Mount Vernon.* Pittsburgh: Beta Phi Mu, 1977.

Carson, James Taylor. *Making an Atlantic World: Circles, Paths, and Stories from the Colonial South.* Knoxville: U of Tennessee P, 2007.

Charron, Pierre. *Of Wisdom: Three Books Written in French.* Trans. Samson Lennard. London: Blount and Aspley, 1625.

———. *Of Wisdom: Three Books Written Originally in French by the Sieur de Charron.* Trans. George Stanhope. 2nd ed. London: R. Bonwick, 1707.

Chauncy, Charles. *Enthusiasm Described and Caution'd Against.* Boston, 1742.

Clarke, Mary T. "The Trinity in Latin Christianity." In *Christian Spirituality: Origins to the Twelfth Century.* Ed. Bernard McGinn and John Meyendorff. New York: Crossroad, 1985.

Clarkson, Thomas. *An Essay on the Slavery and Commerce of the Human Species, Particularly the African.* 1786. Miami, FL: Mnemosyne, 1969.

Clements, Keith W. *Friedrich Schleiermacher: Pioneer of Modern Theology.* London: Collins Liturgical, 1987.

Coffman, Ralph J. *Coleridge's Library: A Bibliography of Books Owned or Read by Samuel Taylor Coleridge.* Boston: G. K. Hall, 1987.

Coleridge, Samuel Taylor. *Biographia Literaria, or Biographical Sketches of My Literary Life and Opinions.* Ed. James Engell and Walter Jackson Bate. 2 vols. in 1. Princeton, NJ: Princeton UP, 1983.

———. *Collected Letters of Samuel Taylor Coleridge: Volume I, 1785–1800.* Ed. Earl Leslie Griggs. Oxford: Oxford UP, 1956.

———. *Lectures 1795 on Politics and Religion.* Ed. Lewis Patton and Peter Mann. Vol. 1 of *The Collected Works of Samuel Taylor Coleridge.* Princeton, NJ: Princeton UP, 1971.

———. *The Notebooks of Samuel Taylor Coleridge: Volume I, 1794–1804.* Part 1, *Text.* Ed. Kathleen Coburn. New York: Pantheon Books, 1957

———. *The Notebooks of Samuel Taylor Coleridge: Volume I, 1794–1804.* Part 2, *Notes.* Ed. Kathleen Coburn. New York: Pantheon Books, 1957.

———. *The Portable Coleridge.* Ed. I. A. Richards. New York: Viking, 1950.

———. *The Watchman.* Ed. Lewis Patton. Vol. 2 of *The Collected Works of Samuel Taylor Coleridge.* Princeton, NJ: Princeton UP, 1970.

Cooper, Anthony Ashley, Third Earl of Shaftsbury. *Characteristicks of Men, Manners, Opinions, Times.* 6th ed. 3 vols. London: J. Purser, 1737–38.

Cooper, David, ed. *A Companion to Aesthetics.* Oxford: Blackwell, 1992.

Copleston, Frederick. *A History of Philosophy.* Part 1 of Vol. 1: *Greece and Rome.* New York: Doubleday, 1946.

———. *A History of Philosophy.* Part 2 of Vol. 1: *Greece and Rome.* New York: Doubleday, 1962

———. *A History of Philosophy.* Part 1 of Vol. 6: *Kant.* Garden City, NY: Doubleday, 1960.

Cunliffe, Marcus. "Thomas Jefferson and the Dangers of the Past." *Wilson Quarterly* 6.1 (Winter 1982): 107.

Dennis, John. *The Critical Works of John Dennis.* Ed. Edward N. Hooker. Vol. 1. Baltimore: Johns Hopkins UP, 1939.

Dewey, Edward H. "Prince, Thomas." *Dictionary of American Biography.* 1935.

Dobson, Michael, gen. ed. *The Oxford Companion to Shakespeare.* New York: Oxford UP, 2001.

Duff, William. *Critical Observations on the Writings of the Most Celebrated Original Geniuses in Poetry.* 1770.

———. *An Essay on Original Genius and Its Various Modes of Exertion in Philosophy and the Fine Arts, Particularly Poetry.* London, 1767.

Edwards, Jonathan. *Treatise Concerning the Religious Affections*. 1746. Ed. John E. Smith. New Haven, CT: Yale UP, 1959.

Eliade, Mircea, gen. ed. *The Encyclopedia of Religion*. 8 vols. New York: Macmillan, 1987.

Elliot, Emory, et al., eds. *Aesthetics in a Multicultural Age*. New York: Oxford UP, 2002.

Ellison, Julie. "The Politics of Fancy in the Age of Sensibility." In *Re-Visioning Romanticism: British Women Writers, 1776–1837*. Ed. Carol S. Wilson and Joel Haefner. Philadelphia: U of Pennsylvania P, 1994. 228–55.

Encyclopedia Britannica. 11th ed. 29 vols. 1911.

Engell, James. *The Creative Imagination: Enlightenment to Romanticism*. Cambridge, MA: Harvard UP, 1981.

Fitzgerald, Allan D., gen. ed. *Augustine through the Ages: An Encyclopedia*. Grand Rapids: Eerdmans, 1999.

Flew, Antony. *A Dictionary of Philosophy*. 2nd ed. New York: St. Martin's, 1984.

Fruman, Norman. *Coleridge, The Damaged Archangel*. New York: George Braziller, 1971.

Fry, Paul H. *Wordsworth and the Poetry of What We Are*. New Haven, CT: Yale UP, 2008.

Fussell, Paul. *Poetic Meter and Poetic Form*. 2nd ed. New York: Random House, 1979.

Gallaway, Francis. *Reason, Rule, and Revolt in English Classicism*. Lexington: U of Kentucky P, 1966.

Gates, Henry Louis, Jr. *Figures in Black: Words, Signs, and the Racial Self*. New York: Oxford UP, 1987.

Gibbons, Sarah. *Kant's Theory of Imagination: Bridging Gaps in Judgment and Experience*. Oxford: Oxford UP, 1994.

Giles, Paul. *Transatlantic Insurrections: British Culture and the Formation of American Literature, 1750–1860*. Philadelphia: U of Pennsylvania P, 2001.

———. *Virtual Americas: Transatlantic Imaginary*. Durham, NC: Duke UP, 2002.

Gordon, Lyndall. *A Life of Mary Wollstonecraft: Vindication*. New York: Harper Collins, 2005.

Gould, Nathaniel D. *Church Music in America*. Boston: A. N. Johnson, 1853. New York: AMS, 1972.

Gray, Jeffrey, ed. *The Greenwood Encyclopedia of American Poets and Poetry*. 5 vols. Westport, CT: Greenwood, 2006

Grégoire, Henri. *An Enquiry Concerning the Intellectual and Moral Faculties and Literature of Negroes*. Trans. P. B. Warden. 1810. College Park, MD: McGrath, 1967.

Hanfmann, George M., and John R. Pollard. "Muses." *The Oxford Classical Dictionary.* Ed. N. G. Hammond and H. H. Scullard. 3rd ed. New York: Oxford UP, 1996.

Harmon, William, and C. Hugh Holman. *A Handbook to Literature.* 10th ed. Upper Saddle River, NJ: Prentice-Hall, 2006.

Hayes, Kevin J., ed. *The Oxford Handbook of Early American Literature.* New York: Oxford UP, 2008.

Hirschfeld, Fritz. *George Washington and Slavery: A Documentary Portrayal.* Columbia: U of Missouri P, 1997.

Hobbes, Thomas. "Answer to Davenant's Preface to *Gondibert.*" In *Critical Essays of the Seventeenth Century.* Ed. J. E. Spingarn. Vol. 2. 1908. Honolulu: UP of the Pacific, 2005. 54–67.

———. *Leviathan.* 1688. Indianapolis: Hackett, 1994.

Hoffmeister, Gerhart, ed. *European Romanticisms: Literary Cross-Currents, Modes, and Models.* Detroit: Wayne State UP, 1990.

Holmes, Richard. *Coleridge: Early Visions.* New York: Penguin, 1990.

Horace. *Ars Poetica.* In *The Critical Tradition: Classic Texts and Contemporary Trends.* Ed. David H. Richter. 2nd ed. Boston: St. Martin's, 1998.

Hyatt, Vera Lawrence, and Rex Nettleford, eds. *Race, Discourse, and the Origin of the Americas: A New World View.* Washington, DC: Smithsonian Institution, 1995.

Imlay, Gilbert. *A Topographical Description of the Western Territory of North America.* 3rd ed. London: Debrett, 1797.

The Interpreter's Bible. General ed. George A. Buttrick. Vol. 5. Nashville: Abingdon, 1956.

Jefferson, Thomas. *Notes on the State of Virginia.* Ed. and intro. Frank Shuffelton. New York: Penguin, 1999.

Jung, Carl G. *Aion: Researches Into the Collective Unconscious.* Trans. R. F. C. Hull. Princeton, NJ: Princeton UP, 1968.

———. *Archetypes and the Collective Unconscious.* Trans. R. F. C. Hull. New York: Pantheon, 1959.

———. "On the Relation of Analytical Psychology to Poetry." In *The Portable Jung.* Ed. Joseph Campbell. New York: Viking, 1971. 301–22.

Kames, Lord, Henry Home. *Elements of Criticism.* 2 vols. 6th ed. 1785. New York: Garland, 1972.

Kant, Immanuel. *Critique of Judgment.* Trans. J. H. Bernard. Macmillan: 1951.

———. *Immanuel Kant: Correspondence.* Trans. Arnulf Zweig. New York: Cambridge UP, 1999.

———. *Observations on the Feeling of the Beautiful and the Sublime.* Trans. T. Goldthwait. Berkeley: U of California P, 1981.

Keats, John. *Complete Poems and Selected Letters.* Ed. Clarence P. Thorpe. New York: Odyssey, 1935.

Kelly, Michael, ed. *Encyclopedia of Aesthetics.* 4 vols. New York: Oxford UP, 1999.

King, William. *An Historical Account of the Heathen Gods and Heroes.* London, 1710.

Kneller, Jane. *Kant and the Power of Imagination.* New York: Cambridge UP, 2007.

Kogel, Renée. *Pierre Charron.* Geneva: Librairie Droz, 1972.

Kors, Alan C., ed. *Encyclopedia of the Enlightenment.* 4 vols. New York: Oxford UP, 2003.

Kuehn, Manfred. *Kant: A Biography.* New York: Cambridge UP, 2001.

Kuncio, Robert C. "Some Unpublished Poems of Phillis Wheatley." *New England Quarterly* 43 (1970): 287–97.

Kyper, Peter Thomas. "The Significance of Mather Byles in the Literary Tradition of America: A Study of His Poems on Several Occasions and His Literary Criticism." PhD diss. Auburn University, 1974.

Lambert, Frank. *Pedlar in Divinity: George Whitefield and the Transatlantic Revivals.* Princeton, NJ: Princeton UP, 1994.

Leclercq, Jean. *The Love of Learning and the Desire for God.* 2nd ed. New York: Fordham UP, 1974.

Levernier, James A., and Douglas R. Wilmes, eds. *American Writers before 1800: A Biographical and Critical Dictionary.* 3 vols. Westport, CT: Greenwood, 1983.

Lewalski, Barbara K. *Protestant Poetics and the Seventeenth-Century Religious Lyric.* Princeton, NJ: Princeton UP, 1979.

Locke, John. *An Essay Concerning Human Understanding.* 4th ed. Ed. Alexander C. Fraser. 2 vols. New York: Dover, 1959.

———. *Some Thoughts Concerning Education.* 1693. Menston, Eng.: Scolar, 1970.

———. *Two Treatises of Government.* Ed. Peter Laslett. 2nd ed. Cambridge: Cambridge UP, 1988.

Longinus. *Peri Houpsos.* In *The Critical Tradition: Classic Texts and Contemporary Trends.* Ed. David H. Richter. 2nd ed. Boston: St. Martin's, 1998.

Lovejoy. Arthur O. *The Great Chain of Being: A Study of the History of an Idea.* Cambridge, MA: Harvard UP, 1964.

Lowes, John Livingston. *The Road to Xanadu: A Study in the Ways of the Imagination.* 2nd ed. Boston: Houghton Mifflin, 1930.

Malof, Joseph. "The Native Rhythm of English Meters." *Texas Studies in Literature and Language* 5 (1964): 580–94.

Martz, Louis. *The Poetry of Meditation: A Study in English Religious Literature of the Seventeenth Century.* New Haven, CT: Yale UP, 1954.

Mason, Julian. "'Ocean': A New Poem by Phillis Wheatley." *Early American Literature* 34 (1999): 78–83.

Mather, Cotton. *The Christian Philosopher.* Ed. Winton Solberg. Chicago: U of Chicago P, 2000.

May, Henry F. *The Enlightenment in America.* New York: Oxford UP, 1976.

McCalman, Iain, gen. ed. *An Oxford Companion to the Romantic Age: British Culture, 1776–1832.* New York: Oxford UP, 1999.

McKay, David, and Richard Crawford. *William Billings of Boston: Eighteenth-Century Composer.* Princeton, NJ: Princeton UP, 1975.

Middlekauff, Robert. *Ancients and Axioms: Secondary Education in Eighteenth-Century New England.* New Haven, CT: Yale UP, 1963.

Monk, Samuel Holt. "'A Grace Beyond the Reach of Art.'" *Journal of the History of Ideas* 5.2 (1944): 131–50.

———. *The Sublime: A Study of Critical Theories in XVIII-Century England.* 2nd ed. Ann Arbor: U of Michigan P, 1960.

Morris, David B. *The Religious Sublime: Christian Poetry and Critical Tradition in Eighteenth-Century England.* Lexington: U of Kentucky P, 1972.

Morrison, Toni. *Playing in the Dark: Whiteness and the Literary Imagination.* Cambridge, MA: Harvard UP, 1992.

Murdock, Kenneth B. "Byles, Mather." *DAB* (1927).

New Interpreter's Bible. Vol. 1. Ed. Terence E. Fretheim. Nashville: Abington P, 1994.

Newlyn, Lucy. *The Cambridge Companion to Coleridge.* New York: Cambridge UP, 2002.

Nochlin, Linda. "Women, Art, and Power." In *Aesthetics.* Ed. Susan L. Feagin and Patrick Maynard. New York: Oxford UP, 1997. 71–78.

Oddell, Margaretta M. "Memoir." In *Memoir and Poems of Phillis Wheatley: A Native African and a Slave. Also, Poems by a Slave.* 3rd ed. 1838. Boston: Mnemosyne, 1969.

Otto, Peter. "Literary Theory." In *An Oxford Companion to the Romantic Age: British Culture, 1776–1832.* Iain McCalman, gen. ed. New York: Oxford UP, 1999. 378–85.

Ovid. *Ovid's Metamorphoses: Books 6–10.* Ed. William S. Anderson. Norman: U of Oklahoma P, 1972.

The Oxford Classical Dictionary. Ed. Simon Hornblower and Anthony Spawforth. 3rd ed. New York: Oxford UP, 1996.

Perkins, William. *A Treatise of Man's Imaginations, Shewing His Naturall Euill Thoughts: His Want of Good Thoughts: The Way to Reforme Them.* Cambridge: John Legat, 1607.

Peterson, Merrill D. "Jefferson, Thomas." *American National Biography.* Ed. John A. Garraty and Mark C. Carnes. Vol. 11. New York: Oxford UP, 1999.

Pietas et Gratulatio (anonymous). Boston: J. Green and J. Russell, 1761.

Plato. *The Works of Plato.* Trans. B. Jowett. New York: Tudor, n.d.

Pope, Alexander. *The Poetry and Prose of Alexander Pope.* Ed. Aubrey Williams. New York: Houghton Mifflin, 1969.

Pourrat, Pierre. *Christian Spirituality.* Vol. 1. London: Burns, Oats, and Washborne, 1922.

Price, Martin. *To the Palace of Wisdom: Studies in Order and Energy from Dryden to Blake.* Carbondale: Southern Illinois UP, 1964.

Rankine, Patrice. *Ulysses in Black: Ralph Ellison, Classicism, and African American Literature.* Madison: U of Wisconsin P, 2006.

Redeker, Martin. *Schleiermacher: Life and Thought.* Philadelphia: Fortress, 1973.

Reynolds, Frances. "Letter to Elizabeth Robinson Montagu," September 10, 1774. In Manuscript located at Harvard University's Houghton Rare Book Library. Call No.: M S Hyde 25.

Reynolds, Joshua. *Discourses on Art.* Ed. Robert R. Wark. San Marino, CA: Huntington Library, 1959.

Rice, Eugene F., Jr. *The Renaissance Idea of Wisdom.* Cambridge, MA: Harvard UP, 1958.

Roberts, Cokie. *Founding Mothers: The Women Who Raised Our Nation.* New York: Harper Collins, 2004.

Robinson, William H. *Black New England Letters: The Uses of Writing in Black New England.* Boston: Trustees of the Public Library of the City of Boston, 1977.

———. *Early Black American Poets: Selections with Biographical and Critical Introductions.* Dubuque, IA: Wm. C. Brown, 1969.

———. *Phillis Wheatley: A Bio-Bibliography.* Boston: Hall, 1981.

———. *Phillis Wheatley in the Black American Beginnings.* Detroit: Broadside, 1975.

———. "Phillis Wheatley: Colonial Quandary." *College Language Association Journal* 9.1 (1965): 25–38.

———. *Phillis Wheatley and Her Writings.* New York: Garland, 1984.

Robinson, William, ed. *Critical Essays on Phillis Wheatley.* Boston: Hall, 1982.

Schleiermacher, Friedrich. *The Christian Faith.* Ed. H. R. Mackintosh and J. S. Stewart. 2 vols. New York: Harper and Row, 1963.

———. *On Religion: Speeches to Its Cultured Despisers.* Trans. John Oman. New York: Harper and Row, 1958.

Seccombe, Joseph. "Business and Diversion Inoffensive to God; and Necessary for the Comfort and Support of Human Society . . . in the Fishing Season." Boston: Kneeland, 1743.

———. *Some Occasional Thoughts on the Influence of the Spirit with Seasonable Cautions against Mistakes and Abuses.* Boston, 1742.

———. *A Specimen of the Harmony of Wisdom and Felicity.* Boston, 1743.

Seeber, Edward Derbyshire. *Anti-Slavery Opinion in France during the Second Half of the Eighteenth Century.* Baltimore: Johns Hopkins UP, 1937; New York: Greenwood, 1969.

Shakespeare, William. *The Riverside Shakespeare.* Gen. ed. G. Blakemore Evans. 2nd ed. Boston: Houghton Mifflin, 1997.

Shaver, Chester L., and Alice C. Shaver. *Wordsworth's Library: A Catalogue, Including a List of Books Housed by Wordsworth for Coleridge from c. 1810 to c. 1830.* New York: Garland, 1979.

Shields, John C. *The American Aeneas: Classical Origins of the American Self.* Knoxville: U of Tennessee P, 2001.

———. "Phillis Wheatley." In *African American Writers.* Ed. Valerie Smith, Lea Baechler, and A. Walton Litz. New York: Charles Scribner's Sons, 1991. 472–91.

———. "Phillis Wheatley and Mather Byles: A Study in Literary Relationship." *College Literature* 23 (June 1980): 377–90.

———. *Phillis Wheatley's Poetics of Liberation: Backgrounds and Contexts.* Knoxville: U of Tennessee P, 2008

———. "Phillis Wheatley and the Sublime." In *Critical Essays on Phillis Wheatley.* Ed. William H. Robinson. Boston: G. K. Hall, 1982. 189–214.

———. "Phillis Wheatley's Subversive Pastoral." *Eighteenth-Century Studies* 27.4 (Summer 1994): 631–47.

Shiner, Carol, and Joel Haefner, eds. *Re-Visioning Romanticism.* Philadelphia: U of Pennsylvania P, 1994.

Sibley, Agnes M. *Alexander Pope's Prestige in America, 1785–1835.* New York: Columbia UP, 1949.

Smith, Valerie, ed. *African American Writers.* 2nd ed. New York: Gale, 2001.

Stedman, John C. *A Narrative of a Five Years' Expedition against the Revolted Negroes of Surinam.* 2 vols. in 1. London: J. J. Johnson, 1796.

Stillinger, Jack, ed. *William Wordsworth: Selected Poems and Prefaces.* Boston: Houghton Mifflin, 1965.

Sunstein, Emily W. *A Different Face: The Life of Mary Wollstonecraft.* New York: Harper and Row, 1975.

Taylor, Edward. *The Poems of Edward Taylor.* Ed. Donald E. Stanford. New Haven, CT: Yale UP, 1960.

Thomson, James. *The Complete Poetical Works.* Ed. J. Logie Robertson. Oxford: Oxford UP, 1908.

Tomalin, Claire. *The Life and Death of Mary Wollstonecraft.* 2nd ed. New York: Penguin, 1992.

Tuveson, Ernest. *The Imagination as a Means of Grace: Locke and the Aesthetics of Romanticism*. Berkeley: U of California P, 1960.

Verhoeven, Wil. *Gilbert Imlay: Citizen of the World*. London: Pickering and Chatto, 2008.

Whale, John. *Imagination under Pressure, 1789–1832: Aesthetics, Politics and Utility*. New York: Cambridge UP, 2000.

Wheatley, Phillis. *The Collected Works of Phillis Wheatley*. Ed. John C. Shields. New York: Oxford UP, 1988.

———. *Letters of Phillis Wheatly [sic], the Negro-Slave Poet of Boston*. Ed. Charles Deane. Boston: J. Wilson and Son, 1864.

Wiersbe, Warren W. "Imagination: The Preacher's Neglected Ally." *Leadership* 4.2 (Spring 1983): 22–27.

Wilson, Ellen Gibson. *Thomas Clarkson: A Biography*. London: Macmillan, 1989.

Witham, W. Tasker. *Living American Literature*. Book 1: *Panorama of American Literature*. New York: Stephen Daye, 1947.

Wordsworth, William. *The Letters of William and Dorothy Wordsworth: The Middle Years*. Ed. Ernest de Selincourt. 2 vols. New York: Oxford UP, 1937.

Yates, Frances A. *Giordano Bruno and the Hermetic Tradition*. Chicago: U of Chicago P, 1964.

Yolton, John W., ed. *The Blackwell Companion to the Enlightenment*. Cambridge, MA: Blackwell, 1991.

Zammito, John H. *The Genesis of Kant's Critique of Judgment*. Chicago: U of Chicago P, 1992.

Zweig, Arnulf, trans. and ed. *Immanuel Kant: Correspondence*. New York: Cambridge UP, 1999.

Index

abolition, 56, 65, 69, 73, 80–88, 99–100, 108
Abrams, Meyer H., 55, 58, 93, 102, 116, 117
Adanson, Michel, *A Voyage to Senegal, the Isle of Greece, and the River Gambia*, 87
Addison, Joseph, 3; *Spectator*, 3, 20, 27, 121
Akenside, Mark, 4; *The Pleasures of Imagination*, 4, 25, 50, 123
Ariosto, Ludovico, 31
Aristotle, 2, 15, 59; *De anima*, 2, 3
Augustine, 1, 5–10, 15, 33, 41, 71; *De trinitate*, 5–6, 7, 8–9

Bacon, Francis, 25
Bate, Walter Jackson, 55, 59
Baym, Max I., 32
beauty, 93, 98
Behn, Aphra, *Oroonoko, or the Royal Slave*, 81
Bell, Archibald, 67
Benezet, Anthony, *Some Historical Account of Guinea . . . with an Inquiry into the Rise and Profess of the Slave Trade*, 87
Biblia Sacra, 11–12
Billings, William, 2, 32, 36–38, 43, 54, 62; "Africa," 37; "America," 37; "Anthem," 36; "Chester," 36; *New-England Psalm-Singer*, 36, 123
Blumenbach, Johann, 65, 73, 108; *Contributions to Natural History*, 68, 84, 88, 108, 124; *On the Natural Variety of Mankind*, 88, 108
Boileau-Despreaux, Nicolas, 4, 39
Bowie, Andrew, 84
Breyfogle, Todd, 6
Brown, Marshall, 55
Brun, Frederica, 115
Bruno, Giordano, 1, 6, 11, 98, 115, 123;
De imaginum signorum et ideasum compositione, 1, 15; *De magia*, 1
Burke, Edmund, 28–29; *Philosphical Enquiry . . .*, 123
Byles, Mather, 2, 7, 15, 25, 32, 38–43, 121; "Eternity," 39; "Hymn to Christ," 41; *Poems on Several Occasions*, 123; "To an Ingenious Young Gentleman. . . ," 40–41; "To Pictorio," 42

Cary, Richard, 67
Charron, Pierre, 2, 20, 38, 43, 46, 90; *De la sagesse*, 2, 20, 22–25, 123
Chauncy, Charles, 32–33; *Enthusiam Described and Caution'd Against*, 33
Cicero, 5–6
Clarkson, Catherine, 68–69
Clarkson, Thomas, 56, 65, 68–69, 116, 121; *An Essay on the Slavery and Commerce of the Human Species, Particularly the African*, 68, 81, 84, 88, 97, 100–101, 123
Coburn, Kathleen, 101
Coleridge, Ernest Hartley, 103
Coleridge, Samuel Taylor, 17, 65, 68, 74, 84, 97, 99–113, 117–18; *Aids to Reflection*, 58; *Biographia Literaria*, 46, 80, 100, 102, 109–13, 115, 118, 124; "Kubla Khan," 101, 107; "Lecture on the Slave Trade," 101, 103; *Lyrical Ballads*, See *Lyrical Ballads*; "Ode to the Slave-Trade," 101; *Poems on Various Subjects*, 102; *Watchman*, 102–6, 124
Cooper, Samuel, 2, 7, 24, 34–35, 36, 43, 54, 122, 123; "A Sermon upon . . . the death of . . . George the Second," 34, 35. See also "Elegy . . . [on the] Learned Samuel Cooper"

Dante, 8; *La commedia*, 8, 40
Dartmouth, Earl of, 77. *See also* "To the ... Earl of Dartmouth"
Davy, Humphry, 108
De Quincey, Thomas, 55, 58, 93
Dennis, John, 25–26
Douglass, Frederick, 56
Dryden, John, 25
Duff, William, *Criticial Observations on the Writings of the Most Celebrated Original Geniuses in Poetry*, 31; *Essay on Original Genius*, 31; *Letters on the Intellectual and Moral Character of Women*, 62

Edwards, Jonathan, 12, 23, 31, 32, 43; *Affections*, 33
"Elegy on Leaving——," 21–22, 62
"Elegy ... [on the] Learned Dr. Samuel Cooper," 36
ekphrasis, 62, 72
Engell, James, 25, 33, 83, 97, 110; *The Creative Imagination*, 19–20, 31–32, 111
epyllion, 8, 107
Equiano, Olaudah, *Interesting Narrative*, 124

Flew, Antony, 55
Franklin, Benjamin, 32
Freneau, Philip, 32, 50
Fricker, Sara, 102
Fruman, Norman, 102–3
"Funeral Poem on the Death of C.E. an Infant of Twelve Months, A," 35

Gallaway, Francis, 55, 66
Gambia, 51, 52, 123
Garrison, William Lloyd, 56
Gates, Henry Louis, Jr., 73, 118–19; *Figures in Black*, 86
Geneva Bible, 11, 16
Gibbons, Sarah, 90, 92
"Goliath of Gath," 29
grammar school, 12, 52, 109
Green, Joseph (the British expatriate in Germany), 86–87, 88
Grégoire, Henri, 65; *De la littérature des négres*, 82
Griggs, Earl L., 108

Hammon, Jupiter, 67
Harmon, William, 55, 117
Harper, Frances Watkins, 122
Harpham, Geoffrey G., 116
Harvard University, 5, 7, 13, 21, 87
Hayes, Kevin J., 32, 122
Herder, Johann, *Ideen zur Philosophie der Geschichte der Menscheit*, 87–88
heterocosm, 31, 50, 51, 53–59, 66–67, 69, 71, 93, 99, 104–7
Hobbes, Thomas, 25; "Answer to Davenant's Preface to *Gondibert*," 25; *Leviathan*, 106, 123
Holman, C. Hugh, 55, 117
Holmes, Richard, 57, 69, 103, 108
Horace, 1, 4, 82; *Ars Poetica*, 4
Hume, David, 73, 86
Huntingdon, Countess of (Selina Hastings), 67
"Hymn to Humanity," 62
"Hymn to the Evening," 68
"Hymn to the Morning," 35, 53, 59, 68, 82, 106

Iliad, 19
Imlay, Gilbert, 65, 89, 116; *Topographical Description of the North American Continent*, 62, 69–73, 89, 100–101, 103, 107, 124
invocation to the muse, 7–8, 48
"Isaiah lxiii," 29, 39–40

Jefferson, Thomas, 32, 70, 82, 116; *Notes on the State of Virginia*, 71
Jerome, Saint, 11

Kames, Lord, Henry Home, 29–30, 35; *Elements of Criticism*, 123
Kant, Immanuel, 30, 65, 85–93, 109; "Analytic of the Sublime," 29, 51, 57, 75, 93; *The Critique of Judgment*, 85, 88, 89, 91–93, 97, 110, 124; *Critique of Pure Reason*, 90; *Observations on the Feeling of the Beautiful and Sublime*, 73, 86, 89
Keats, John, 29, 47, 67; *Endymion*, 45; "Ode to a Nightingale," 42, 54
King James Bible, 11, 77, 106

King, William, *An Historical Account of the Heathen Gods and Heroes*, 52
Kneller, Jane, 90–91, 94, 97
Kuehn, Manfred, 85–87
Kyper, Peter T., 19

Lecointe-Marsillac, 81
Lavallée, Joseph, *Le Nègre comme il y a peu de Blancs*, 81
"Letter of Attestation," 33, 67, 68, 100
Lewalski, Barbara Kiefer, 7
"Liberty and Peace," 34
Longinus, 1, 4–5, 15, 26, 50; *Peri hupsous (On the Sublime)*; 4–5, 39
"Long Poem," 45, 55, 60, 62, 65, 66–67, 72, 89, 98, 99, 112, 117
Lovejoy, Arthur O., 86
Lowes, John Livingston, 107, 112
Loyola, Ignatius, 6–7
Lyrical Ballads, 69, 75, 124

Martz, Louis L., 6–7
McCalman, Iain, 55, 115–16
meditatio, 5–8, 26, 47–48, 49, 116
memory, 2–3, 5, 7–10, 24, 28, 38, 41, 45, 47–49, 59–60, 72, 78, 89, 99
Middle Passage, 45, 47, 110
Milton, John, 8, 35, 109; *Paradise Lost*, 8, 39, 87
Monk, Samuel Holt, 27
Montagu, Elizabeth Robinson, 121
Moore, Hannah (the Brit), 68
Morehead, Scipio, 4. *See also* "To S.M. a Young African Painter, on Seeing His Works"
Morris, David, 26
Motherby, Robert, 87

New England Weekly Journal, 40, 41
"Niobe in Distress . . . ," 8, 29, 62, 72, 107
Nochlin, Linda, 115

Occom, Samson, 56, 123
Oddell, Margaretta M., 99
Odiorne, Thomas, *Progress of Refinement*, 122

Old South Church, 21, 98
"On Being Brought from Africa," 3
"On Imagination," 4, 6, 10, 17, 20, 27–28, 30–31, 37, 41–43, 45, 49–54, 60, 66, 69, 74–80, 88, 91, 97–99, 101, 103, 104–7
"On Messrs. Hussey and Coffin," 123
"On Recollection," 14, 24, 45–47, 51, 59–60, 66, 91, 107, 110, 113
"On the Death of J.C. an Infant," 82
"On the Death of the Rev. Geroge Whitefield," 123
Otto, Peter, 55, 58, 60, 66, 67

Pentateuch, 2, 10–11
Perkins, William, 12
Pietas et Gratulatio, 32, 34–35, 123
Plato, 2, 3, 5; *Ion*, 2, 15; *Republic*, 2; *Phadedrus*, 2
Plato, Ann, 122
Poe, Edgar Allan, 119, 122
Pope, Alexander, 1, 19–20, 35, 76, 77; "Epistle to Bathurst," 53; *Essay on Criticism*, 19; *An Essay on Man*, 20

reason. *See* understanding
Renaissance, 1–2, 6, 8, 46
Reynolds, Frances, 68, 121
Rice, Eugene F., Jr., 22
Roberts, Cokle, 119
Robertson, J. Logie, 76
Robinson, Mary ("Perdita"), 115

Schelling, Friedrich, 110–14
Schleiermacher, Friedrich, 83–84, 89; *The Christian Faith*, 83;*On Religion: Speeches to Its Cultured Despisers*, 73, 83
Schweitzer, Madeleine, 73
Seccombe, Joseph, 2, 20–24, 32–33, 43, 90, 123; *A Specimen of the Harmony of Wisdom and Felicity*, 48; *Some Occasional Thoughts*, 22; "Ye Happy Fields," 21–22
Sewall, Joseph, 20–21, 37
Sewall, Samuel, 20
Shaftsbury, Third Earl of (Anthony Ashley Cooper), 26–27; *Characteristics of Men, Manners, Opinions, Times*, 123

Shakespeare, William, 2, 13, 15, 35, 109; *Henry VIII*, 14, 47; *Julius Ceasar*, 13–14, 109; *A Midsummer Night's Dream*, 2, 13–17; *Venus and Adonis*, 112
Sharp, Granville, 56
Shelley, 83
Shields, John, *Phillis Wheatley's Poetics of Liberation*, 8, 9, 13, 14, 57, 58, 61, 67, 99, 115
Singing Schools, 36, 37
slavery, 10, 14, 36, 41, 43, 46–60, 65–74, 76, 80–82, 89, 92, 94, 98–105, 121
sophrosyne, 2, 26
Southey, Robert, 100, 101
Stanhope, George, 24
Stedman, John C., 116; *Narrative of a Five Year's Expedition against the Revolted Negroes of Surinam*, 73–74, 101
Stewart, Dugald, *Elements of the Philosophy of the Human Mind*, 97
Stillinger, Jack, 55, 75, 79, 93, 117–18
sublime, 26–31, 33–35, 39–40, 51, 57, 74–75, 77, 79, 85, 99, 103, 112, 118, 122

Tanner, Obour, 61
Taylor, Edward, 6–7; *Poetic Meditations*, 7
Terence, 71
Thomson, James, 76–77; *Liberty*, 77; *The Seasons*, 76
Thornton, John, 67
"Thoughts on the Works of Providence," 3, 5, 7, 8–10, 25, 30, 39, 41, 45, 47–49, 57, 66, 78, 91, 106, 110, 113, 116
"To the . . . Earl of Dartmouth," 56, 82
"To George Washington," 34
"To Maecenas," 55–56, 62, 82
"To S.M. a Young African Painter, on seeing His Works," 4, 62, 72, 107
"To the University of Cambridge in New England," 13, 109

Tyler, Moses Coit, 32
Tyndale, William, 2, 10–13, 71

understanding, 5, 7–11, 20, 29, 35, 41, 47, 49, 89–93, 113
Uyl, Douglas Den, 26

Vergil, 21, 51, 109; eclogues, 46, 47
Verhoeven, Wil, 70, 103
Voltaire, François Arouet de, 81, 116

Warren, Mercy Otis, 119
Watson, Brook, 87
Whale, John, 53, 55, 67
Wheatley, John, 51, 56, 87
Wheatley, Phillis, 1, 3–5, 7–10, 12–14; and Christianity, 6, 10, 13, 57, 67; liberation poetics, 38, 43, 46, 51–52, 72; literary influences, 2, 7; manumission of, 56, 61, 76, 123; *Poems on Various Subjects, Religious and Moral*, 1, 23, 53, 61, 66, 69, 76, 81, 100, 102, 108, 121, 123; religious freedom, 57, 62, 65–67
Wheatley, Susannah, 37, 51
Whitefield, George, 22–23, 33
Wiersbe, Warren W., 12–13
will, 2–3, 7, 8, 9, 10, 41, 47, 49, 111
Wollstonecraft, Mary, 62, 69, 73, 89
women's rights, 62, 65
Woodward, William W., 81
Wooster, David, 61, 123
Wordsworth, Dorothy, 68
Wordsworth, William, 9, 10, 60, 68–69, 74–80, 100, 117–18, 121; *Lyrical Ballads*, See *Lyrical Ballads*; *Prelude*, 45, 75, 78–79

Zammito, John H., 87
Zweig, Arnulf, 88, 94